Makin...
Wor...

ALSO AVAILABLE

Making MS-DOS
Work For You

by

N. Kantaris
and
P.R.M. Oliver

BERNARD BABANI (publishing) LTD.
THE GRAMPIANS
SHEPHERDS BUSH ROAD
LONDON W6 7NF
ENGLAND

PLEASE NOTE

Although every care has been taken with the production of this book to ensure that any projects, designs, modifications and/or programs, etc., contained herewith, operate in a correct and safe manner and also that any components specified are normally available in Great Britain, the Publishers and Author(s) do not accept responsibility in any way for the failure (including fault in design) of any project, design, modification or program to work correctly or to cause damage to any equipment that it may be connected to or used in conjunction with, or in respect of any other damage or injury that may be so caused, nor do the Publishers accept responsibility in any way for the failure to obtain specified components.

Notice is also given that if equipment that is still under warranty is modified in any way or used or connected with home-built equipment then that warranty may be void.

© 1992 BERNARD BABANI (publishing) LTD

First Published — November 1992
Reprinted — August 1993

British Library Cataloguing in Publication Data

Kantaris, Noel
    Making MS-DOS Work for You
    I. Title II. Oliver, Phil
    005.4

ISBN 0 85934 319 7

Printed and Bound in Great Britain by Cox & Wyman Ltd, Reading

ABOUT THIS BOOK

Making MS-DOS Work for You has been written for those who already have some knowledge of MS/PC-DOS commands, but who would like to be able to write customised batch files, create specialist programs with the use of the **debug** program and, in general, extend their abilities towards designing and setting up their own professional looking menus so that they or others could run any program application or package easily.

The book was not designed to teach you how to use DOS commands in a routine manner. If you need to know about this aspect of DOS, then may we suggest that you also refer to either the book *A Concise Introduction to MS-DOS* (BP232) if you are a pre-DOS 5 user, or *A Concise User's Guide to MS-DOS 5* (BP318) if you use DOS 5, or *MS-DOS 6 Explained* (BP341) if you use DOS 6. These books are also published by the BERNARD BABANI (publishing) LTD and one of these might be more appropriate for you at this stage with its lower entry point into DOS.

This book was written with the busy person in mind. It is not necessary to read hundreds of pages to find out all there is to know about a subject, when a few pages can do the same thing quite adequately! With the help of this book, it is hoped that you will be able to get the most out of your computer in terms of efficiency, productivity and enjoyment, and that you will be able to do it in the shortest, most effective and informative way.

If you would like to purchase a floppy disc containing all the programs which appear in this, or any other listed book(s) by the same author(s), then fill-in the form at the back of the book and send it to P. Oliver at the stipulated address.

ABOUT THE AUTHORS

Noel Kantaris graduated in Electrical Engineering at Bristol University and after spending three years in the Electronics Industry in London, took up a Tutorship in Physics at the University of Queensland. Research interests in Ionospheric Physics, led to the degrees of M.E. in Electronics and Ph.D. in Physics. On return to the UK, he took up a Post-Doctoral Research Fellowship in Radio Physics at the University of Leicester, and in 1973 a Senior Lectureship in Engineering at The Camborne School of Mines, Cornwall, where since 1978 he has also assumed the responsibility of Head of Computing.

Phil Oliver graduated in Mining Engineering at Camborne School of Mines in 1967 and since then has specialised in most aspects of surface mining technology, with a particular emphasis on computer related techniques. He has worked in Guyana, Canada, several Middle Eastern countries, South Africa and the United Kingdom, on such diverse projects as: The planning and management of bauxite, iron, gold and coal mines; rock excavation contracting in the U.K.; international mining equipment sales and technical back up; international mine consulting for a major mining house in South Africa. In 1988 he took up a Senior Lectureship at Camborne School of Mines in Surface Mining and Management.

ACKNOWLEDGEMENTS

We would like to thank colleagues at the Camborne School of Mines for the helpful tips and suggestions which assisted us in the writing of this book.

TRADEMARKS

CONTENTS

1. INTRODUCTION

When you switch on your IBM compatible PC it will first perform some memory test procedures, then, depending on your set-up, it may print some lines of proprietary text on the screen, and finally will leave you with a basic DOS prompt, such as:

```
C:\>
```

All of this will almost certainly be in a boring white text on a black background. This is neither very inspiring nor very user friendly.

On the other hand most commercial software is designed with 'user-friendly' screens incorporating such attributes as reverse video and colour, and with information appearing in the right place on the screen. MS-DOS can also be made to do just this, provided you know how. To this end, you will be shown how to write specialized batch files with the use of the **Edit** screen editor or the **Edlin** line editor, and how to design your own screen menus like the one below. You could, of course, buy a commercial program that could do this, but then it would cost you more, you would not learn anything new, nor have anywhere near as much fun.

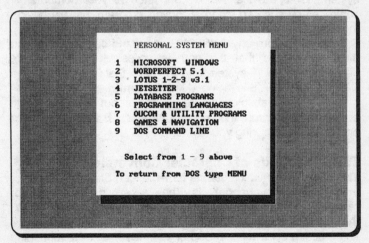

Which editor you use to write these specialized files will depend largely on which version of DOS you are using, with pre-DOS 5

users being restricted to the use of **Edlin**. However, for the sake of completeness, both these editors will be fully explained; **Edit** in Chapter 2 and **Edlin** in Chapter 3. There are also many other commercial text editors available, such as the Norton Editor. If you have one of these we will assume that you are familiar with its use. Text editors can be used to write simple batch files to allow you to easily run an application, but creating a professional looking batch file requires you to write some specialised, but small, programs in assembler. For those who would like to know more about how this is done, the **Debug** program is explained in Appendix A.

However, provided you can handle one of the editors, you will be shown how to extend your abilities towards designing and setting up your own professional looking menu screens so that you, or others, can choose and run program applications or packages easily on your system, without having to become an expert assembler programmer.

Although the internal DOS commands provide control over the disc drives and, to a lesser extent, control over the keyboard and display screen, the appearance of the screen can be controlled far more effectively with the ANSI.SYS driver. This is an external program supplied with your MS-DOS operating system. Every device that is connected to your computer is controlled by such an external "driver" program, usually having the filename extension SYS.

However, before any ANSI.SYS command can be used, you must make sure that the path is accessible from the root directory of your system's disc and that the extra line DEVICE=ANSI.SYS is included in your **config.sys** file.

If you are not absolutely sure what is meant by the contents of the last paragraph, then refer to Appendix B which discusses one way of configuring your system.

The ASCII Code of Character Conversion
The ASCII code (which stands for American Standard Code for Information Interchange) is the accepted standard for representing characters in computers. It defines codes 0 to 127; the first 32 (codes 0 to 31) as control characters, which define some action such as line-feed or form-feed, and the remaining (codes 32 to 127) as standard characters which normally appear on a computer keyboard. Since each byte can represent

one of 256 possible characters, there are another 128 codes available (codes 128 to 255) for which, however, there is no formal standard laid down. These codes are used by IBM and IBM compatibles and are known as the IBM extended character set.

The IBM extended character set includes four main groups:

a) Accented international characters (codes 128 to 168);
b) Line drawing characters (codes 169 to 223);
c) Greek letters (codes 224 to 239), and
d) Mathematical symbols (codes 240 to 254).

All the codes are shown in the ASCII Conversion Codes table which appears in the following pages. The table shows all 256 characters and tabulates their values in both decimal (base 10) and hexadecimal (base 16) representation. All, but one, ASCII codes can be entered into the computer by holding the key marked <Alt> down and typing the decimal character code on the numeric keypad (not the numbers appearing on the first row of keys of the normal keyboard. On releasing the <Alt> key, the corresponding character appears on the screen. Thus, typing

```
C:\> Alt+236
```

causes the symbol for infinity (∞) to appear on the screen.

The one character code that can not be entered with this method is the 'null' character (code 0). To enter this character, which will appear as ^@ on your screen, press **F7** while at the DOS prompt, or while using **Edlin** or the **Debug** program (the last one of which will be discussed in some detail later). To enter the same character while using **Edit**, first press the Ctrl+P key combination, then press <Esc> followed by the <@> key.

The first 32 character codes (0 to 31) can also be entered with the <Ctrl> key, as indicated in the ASCII Conversion Codes table. Using this method, however, causes DOS to echo the caret (^) character followed by the corresponding letter on the screen. **Edlin**, like DOS, allows you to enter the control characters with either the <Ctrl> key or the <Alt> key, but always echoes a caret followed by the appropriate letter.

TABLE 1 ASCII Conversion Codes

CHAR	ABBR	DEC	HEX	CHAR	ABBR	DEC	HEX	CHAR	ABBR	DEC	HEX
CTRL @	nul	0	00	CTRL K	vt	11	0B	CTRL V	syn	22	16
CTRL A	soh	1	01	CTRL L	ff	12	0C	CTRL W	etb	23	17
CTRL B	stx	2	02	CTRL M	cr	13	0D	CTRL X	can	24	18
CTRL C	etx	3	03	CTRL N	so	14	0E	CTRL Y	em	25	19
CTRL D	eot	4	04	CTRL O	si	15	0F	CTRL Z	sub	26	1A
CTRL E	enq	5	05	CTRL P	dle	16	10	CTRL [	esc	27	1B
CTRL F	ack	6	06	CTRL Q	dc1	17	11	CTRL \	fs	28	1C
CTRL G	bel	7	07	CTRL R	dc2	18	12	CTRL]	gs	29	1D
CTRL H	bs	8	08	CTRL S	dc3	19	13	CTRL ^	rs	30	1E
CTRL I	ht	9	09	CTRL T	dc4	20	14	CTRL _	us	31	1F
CTRL J	lf	10	0A	CTRL U	nak	21	15				
SPACE		32	20	@		64	40	`		96	60
!		33	21	A		65	41	a		97	61
"		34	22	B		66	42	b		98	62
#		35	23	C		67	43	c		99	63
$		36	24	D		68	44	d		100	64
%		37	25	E		69	45	e		101	65
&		38	26	F		70	46	f		102	66
'		39	27	G		71	47	g		103	67
(		40	28	H		72	48	h		104	68
)		41	29	I		73	49	i		105	69
*		42	2A	J		74	4A	j		106	6A
+		43	2B	K		75	4B	k		107	6B
,		44	2C	L		76	4C	l		108	6C
-		45	2D	M		77	4D	m		109	6D
.		46	2E	N		78	4E	n		110	6E
/		47	2F	O		79	4F	o		111	6F
0		48	30	P		80	50	p		112	70
1		49	31	Q		81	51	q		113	71
2		50	32	R		82	52	r		114	72
3		51	33	S		83	53	s		115	73
4		52	34	T		84	54	t		116	74
5		53	35	U		85	55	u		117	75
6		54	36	V		86	56	v		118	76
7		55	37	W		87	57	w		119	77
8		56	38	X		88	58	x		120	78
9		57	39	Y		89	59	y		121	79
:		58	3A	Z		90	5A	z		122	7A
;		59	3B	[		91	5B	{		123	7B
<		60	3C	\		92	5C	|		124	7C
=		61	3D	]		93	5D	}		125	7D
>		62	3E	^		94	5E	~		126	7E
?		63	3F	_		95	5F	del		127	7F

TABLE 1 (Contd)

CHAR	DEC	HEX	CHAR	DEC	HEX	CHAR	DEC	HEX
Ç	128	80	½	171	AB		214	D6
ü	129	81	¼	172	AC		215	D7
é	130	82	¡	173	AD		216	D8
â	131	83	«	174	AE		217	D9
ä	132	84	»	175	AF		218	DA
à	133	85		176	B0		219	DB
å	134	86		177	B1		220	DC
ç	135	87		178	B2		221	DD
ê	136	88		179	B3		222	DE
ë	137	89		180	B4		223	DF
è	138	8A		181	B5	α	224	E0
ï	139	8B		182	B6	ß	225	E1
î	140	8C		183	B7	Γ	226	E2
ì	141	8D		184	B8	π	227	E3
Ä	142	8E		185	B9	Σ	228	E4
Å	143	8F		186	BA	σ	229	E5
É	144	90		187	BB	µ	230	E6
æ	145	91		188	BC	τ	231	E7
Æ	146	92		189	BD	Φ	232	E8
ô	147	93		190	BE	Θ	233	E9
ö	148	94		191	BF	Ω	234	EA
ò	149	95		192	C0	δ	235	EB
û	150	96		193	C1	∞	236	EC
ù	151	97		194	C2	φ	237	ED
ÿ	152	98		195	C3	ε	238	EE
Ö	153	99		196	C4	∩	239	EF
Ü	154	9A		197	C5	≡	240	F0
¢	155	9B		198	C6	±	241	F1
£	156	9C		199	C7	≥	242	F2
¥	157	9D		200	C8	≤	243	F3
₧	158	9E		201	C9	⌠	244	F4
ƒ	159	9F		202	CA	⌡	245	F5
á	160	A0		203	CB	÷	246	F6
í	161	A1		204	CC	≈	247	F7
ó	162	A2		205	CD	°	248	F8
ú	163	A3		206	CE	∙	249	F9
ñ	164	A4		207	CF	·	250	FA
Ñ	165	A5		208	D0	√	251	FB
ª	166	A6		209	D1	ⁿ	252	FC
º	167	A7		210	D2	²	253	FD
¿	168	A8		211	D3	■	254	FE
⌐	169	A9		212	D4		255	FF
¬	170	AA		213	D5			

2. THE MS-DOS EDITOR

MS-DOS provides you with a full screen editor, called **Edit**, with which you can create special ASCII files to customise your system. These are text files which, when sent to the screen or printer, are interpreted as text, unlike the .COM or .EXE files which are binary files.

Edit can also be used to create the source code of various programming languages, such as Fortran and C. In such cases, do remember to give the files the appropriate extension, which for the two languages mentioned, are **.for** and **.c**, respectively.

To invoke **Edit**, the MS-DOS system start-up disc or a disc that contains it, must be accessible and the full path of the file you want to create or edit must be specified. Thus, typing the command:

```
C:\>edit test.txt
```

expects to find both **Edit** and the fictitious file **test.txt** on the disc in the logged drive (in this case C:), while typing

```
C:\>edit A:test.txt
```

expects to find **Edit** on the C: drive, and the file **test.txt** on the disc in the A: drive.

If the file does not exist on the specified disc or directory, then **Edit** displays a blank screen, as follows:

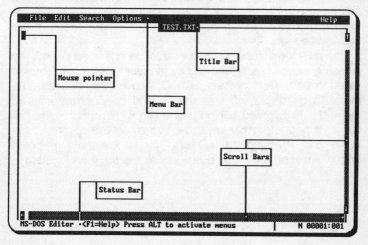

7

The **Edit** screen is subdivided into several areas which have the following function:

Area	Function
Menu bar	allows you to choose from several main menu options
Title bar	displays the name of the current file. If a new file, it displays the word <Untitled>
Status bar	displays the current file status and information regarding the present process
Scroll bar	allows you to scroll the screen with the use of the mouse.

The area bounded by the Title bar and the two Scroll bars is known as the view window. It is in this area that you enter the contents of a new file, or load and view the contents of an old file.

The Editor Menu Bar

Each menu bar option on the editor, has associated with it a pull-down sub-menu. To activate the menu bar, either press the <Alt> key, which causes the first item on the menu bar (in this case **File**) to be highlighted, then use the right and left arrow keys to highlight any of the items of the menu bar, or use the mouse to point to an item. Pressing either the <Enter> key, or the left mouse button, reveals the pull-down sub-menu of the highlighted menu item.

The pull-down sub-menus can also be activated directly by pressing the <Alt> key followed by the first letter of the required menu option. Thus pressing **Alt+O**, causes the Options submenu to be displayed. Use the up and down arrow keys to move the highlighted bar up and down within a sub-menu, or the right and left arrow keys to move along the options of the menu bar. Pressing the <Enter> key selects the highlighted option, while pressing the <Esc> key closes the menu system.

The Menu Bar Options:
Each item of the menu bar offers the options described below. However, dimmed command names in the **Edit** sub-menu indicate that these commands are unavailable at this time; you might need to select some text before you can use them.

The information given below can be displayed by highlighting the required sub-menu option and pressing the **F1** help key. This information is listed here for easier reference.

The File Sub-Menu
Selecting **File** causes the following pull-down sub-menu to be displayed:

New: Use to create a new document file.

Open: Use to open an existing document so you can edit or print it.

Save: Use to save the current version of your document.

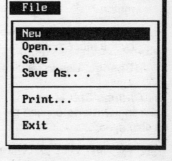

Save As: Use to save your document as a file.
To preserve the previous version of your document, rename it in the File Name dialogue box.

Print: Use to print all or part of a document.

Exit: Use to quit the MS-DOS Editor environment.

The Edit Sub-Menu
Selecting **Edit** causes the following pull-down sub-menu to be displayed:

Cut: Use to remove selected text and put it on the Clipboard, a temporary holding area.

Copy: Use to copy selected text to the Clipboard. The original text remains unchanged.

Paste: Use to insert a block of text from the Clipboard at any point in a document.

Clear: Use to delete selected text without copying it to the Clipboard, whose contents remain unchanged.

The Search Sub-Menu

Selecting **Search** causes the following pull-down sub-menu to be displayed:

Find: Use to search for a text string. You can request a case-sensitive match or a whole-word match.

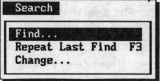

Repeat Last Find: Use to repeat the search performed by the most recent Find or Change command.

Change: Use to replace one text string with another.

The Options Sub-Menu:

Selecting **Options** causes the following pull-down sub-menu to be displayed:

Display: Use to control screen colour, scroll bars in windows, and the number of spaces <Tab> advances the cursor.

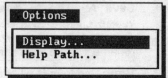

Help Path: Use to change the directories that the MS-DOS Editor searches to find the Help file EDIT.HLP

Help Menu

Selecting **Help** causes the following pull-down sub-menu to be displayed:

Getting Started: Use to find out about using MS-DOS Editor menus, commands, and dialogue boxes. Also to get Help on using the Editor.

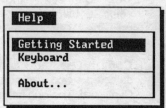

10

Keyboard: Use to find out about keystrokes for performing tasks on the MS-DOS Editor, and the WordStar keystrokes that can be used with the Editor.

About: Use to display the version number and copyright information for the MS-DOS Editor.

Dialogue Boxes:

Three periods after a sub-menu option, means that a dialogue box will open when the option is selected. A dialogue box is used for the insertion of additional information, such as the name of a file to be opened, or to be acted upon in some way.

To understand dialogue boxes, type the word 'hi' in the edit screen, then press **Alt+S**, and select the **Change** option from the revealed sub-menu of **Search**. The dialogue box shown below will now appear on the screen.

```
┌──────────────────────── Change ─────────────────────────┐
│                                                          │
│   Find What: ┌────────────────────────────────────────┐ │
│              │hi                                        │ │
│              └────────────────────────────────────────┘ │
│                                                          │
│   Change To: ┌────────────────────────────────────────┐ │
│              │hello                                     │ │
│              └────────────────────────────────────────┘ │
│                                                          │
│                                                          │
│      [ ] Match Upper/Lowercase        [ ] Whole Word     │
│                                                          │
│ ╣ Find and Verify ╠ < Change All > < Cancel > < Help >   │
└──────────────────────────────────────────────────────────┘
```

The <Tab> key can be used to move the cursor from one field to another within a dialogue box, while the <Enter> key is only used to indicate that the options within the various fields within the dialogue box are specified correctly. Every dialogue box contains one field which is enclosed in emboldened angle-brackets (<Find and Verify>, in the above example). This field indicates the action that **Edit** will take if the <Enter> key is pressed (in our example, the word 'hi' will be changed to 'hello', if this is what we choose to type against the 'Find What' and 'Change To' fields.

Pressing the <Esc> key aborts the menu option and returns you to the editor.

11

Moving About the Screen:

The cursor can be moved to any part of the text being typed in the view window, and corrections can be made, with the use of the key strokes described below.

Key	Function
Left Arrow	moves cursor to the left one character
Right Arrow	moves cursor to the right one character
Ctrl+Left Arrow	moves cursor to the beginning of the previous word on the current line
Ctrl+Right Arrow	moves cursor to the beginning of the next word on the current line
Home	moves cursor to the first column of the current line
End	move cursor to the end of the last word on the current line
Up Arrow	moves cursor up one line
Down Arrow	moves cursor down one line
Ctrl+Home	moves cursor to the first line of the current screen
Ctrl+End	moves cursor to the last line of the current screen
PgUp	moves cursor to the previous screen
PgDn	moves cursor to the next screen
Ctrl+PgUp	moves cursor left one screen
Ctrl+PgDn	moves cursor right one screen
Ins	toggles the Insert mode from ON (its default position) to OFF and back again
Enter	moves cursor to the beginning of the next line, provided the insert mode is in the ON position
Ctrl+Y	deletes the line at the current cursor position
Ctrl+N	inserts a blank line at the current cursor position
Shift+Arrows	marks block areas on the screen to be used with the sub-menu of the Edit option, namely Cut, Copy, Past, and Clear.

When areas of text are marked, with either the use of the **Shift+Arrows** or by clicking and dragging the mouse, **Edit** keeps the contents of the blocked (highlighted) area of text in a temporary storage area known as the 'clipboard' from which it can be retrieved later when the **Cut**, **Copy**, and **Paste** options are used. The Clipboard stores only one block of information at a time. If you attempt to store a second block of information, it simply overrides the previously stored block.

If you are not using a mouse, you might want to clear the scroll bars from the screen, to give you more room. This can be done by pressing **Alt+O**, selecting the **Display** option and pressing the <Tab> key until the cursor is positioned in the 'Scroll Bars' field. Pressing the spacebar toggles the option into the off position by clearing the letter X from within the square brackets.

If you are using a mouse scrolling text in the view window is easy. Place the mouse pointer on the top, bottom, left or right of the scroll bars and click the left mouse button to scroll upwards, downwards, to the left or to the right, respectively.

There are a lot more commands associated with **Edit**, but you'll find that the ones given above are sufficient for almost all your needs.

Creating & Saving a Text File

As an example, type the following lines in **Edit**'s view window:

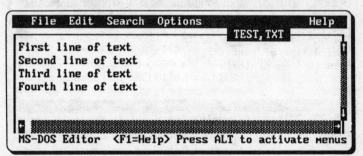

Editing Text:

To edit any part of the document, use the up or down arrow keys to place the cursor at the beginning of the line you want to edit, then use the right or left arrow keys to place the cursor at the required position where you want to begin editing.

If you have a mouse, simply point to the place you want to edit and click the left mouse button to place the cursor at the position occupied by the mouse pointer.

Use one of the above techniques to change the second line of our document to

```
Second line of text, edited
```

Selecting Text:
To select text, place the cursor at the required starting position, and while holding down the <Shift> key, press the right or left arrow keys to highlight as much of the text on that line as you like. With the mouse, place the mouse pointer at the required starting position and while holding down the left mouse button, move the mouse horizontally to the right or left to highlight the required text on that line.

If you try to select text which runs to more than one line, the whole line (first and subsequent) will be selected. Thus, you can either select text from part of a line, or you select text from whole lines.

As an example, select the words ' of text' (including the leading space) from the second line, as shown below:

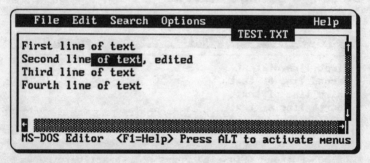

Moving Text:
Having selected the part of text you want to move, use the **Edit, Cut** command, then place the cursor at the required point where you would like to move the text to, and use the **Edit, Paste** command.

As an example, select the words ' of text' (including the leading space) from the second line, then use the **Edit, Cut,**

followed by the **Edit, Paste** commands, to move the selected
text to the end of the fourth line. The result is shown below:

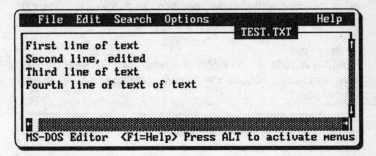

Clearing Text:

To remove text from a document without changing the contents
of the Clipboard, highlight the unwanted text, then use the **Edit,
Clear** command.

   Use this command to remove from the fourth line both
repetitions of the words 'of text', then, to prove that the contents
of the Clipboard have not changed, use the **Edit, Paste**
command to restore the fourth line to its original form.

   In fact, you can paste the contents of the Clipboard to any
part of a document, as many times as you like, because pasting
does not empty the Clipboard.

Copying Text:

To copy text, highlight the required text, then use the **Edit,
Copy** command.

   Use this command to copy the whole of the second line to the
Clipboard, then use the **Edit, Paste** command, to paste a copy
of it on to the fifth line of the document. Next, change the words
'Second' to 'Fifth' and 'edited' to 'added', as shown.

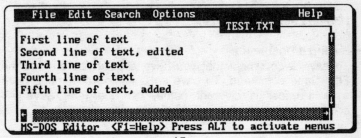

You will have to use the <Del> key to delete the unwanted words as the editor is normally in 'insert' mode and when typing text it inserts it at the cursor position. To toggle the edit mode from 'insert' to 'overtype', press the <Ins> key once.

Finding Text:
To find a specific word or part of a word, use the **Search, Find** command which causes the following dialogue box to appear on your screen:

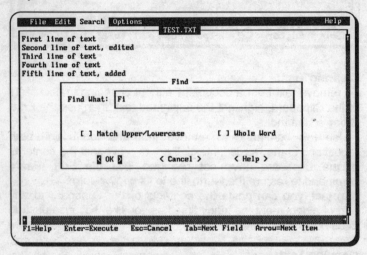

Note that the word nearest to the cursor is offered in the 'Find What' field as a default. In the above example, if the cursor is at the beginning of the document, the default word will be 'First'.

   As an example, to find all the words that begin with the letters 'Fi', after typing these in the 'Find What' field, press the <**OK**> button. **Edit** highlights the first word containing these letters, and to find the next occurrence you will have to use the **Search, Repeat Last Find** command.

Saving a Document:
To save a document that you have already named, use the **File, Save** command. To save an unnamed document, or to save it under a different name, use the **File, Save As** command.

Selecting this last command, causes the following dialogue box to appear on your screen:

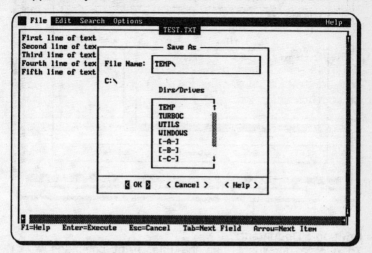

Note that you can save a document to any subdirectory or drive by selecting appropriately from the Dirs/Drives list within the dialogue box.

Opening a Document:
Once a document has been saved to a file on disc, you can open it by using the **File, Open** command which causes the dialogue box shown on the next page to appear on your screen.

Again, you can select any of the **.txt** files (which is the default file extension) from the logged drive and subdirectory, or indeed change the extension to, say, **.bat** if you want to work with batch files such as the **autoexec.bat** file.

Also note that you can change the logged directory or drive by selecting appropriately from the Dirs/Drives list within the dialogue box.

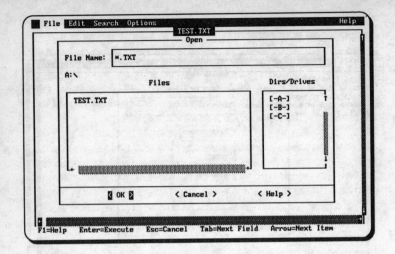

```
  ■ File  Edit  Search  Options                              Help
                          ┌──TEST.TXT──┐
                         ─┤   Open    ├─
     File Name: ┌─────────────────────────────────────────┐
                │ *.TXT                                     │
                └─────────────────────────────────────────┘
     A:\
                     Files                     Dirs/Drives
     ┌──────────────────────────────────┐  ┌───────────────┐
     │ TEST.TXT                          │  │ [-A-]       ↑ │
     │                                   │  │ [-B-]         │
     │                                   │  │ [-C-]       ▓ │
     │                                   │  │             ▓ │
     │                                   │  │               │
     │ └─ ▒▒▒▒▒▒▒▒▒▒▒▒▒▒▒▒▒▒▒▒▒▒▒▒▒─┘    │  │             ↓ │
     └──────────────────────────────────┘  └───────────────┘

              █ OK █          < Cancel >          < Help >

  ■ F1=Help  Enter=Execute  Esc=Cancel  Tab=Next Field  Arrow=Next Item
```

Printing a Document:

To print a document, use the **File, Print** command which causes the 'Print' dialogue box to appears on your screen

Note that you can choose to print the complete document (which is the default setting) in the dialogue box, or a pre-selected part of the document. If you are printing the whole document, simply press the <**OK**> button, but if you are printing a selected part of the document (which must have been selected before initiating the **File, Print** command), then choose the 'Selected Text Only' option from the dialogue box.

The **Print** command works only if you have a printer connected to or redirected through your parallel printer port (LPT1).

Exiting the Editor

To end the current session and exit **Edit**, select the **File** menu and choose the **Exit** option from the revealed sub-menu.

If you were working with a new file or a file that had been changed but not saved, **Edit** will prompt you to save it before exiting.

3. THE EDLIN LINE EDITOR

MS-DOS provides you with a simple line editor, called **Edlin**, and it is worth becoming familiar with its use. In general, **Edlin** allows the creation and editing of ASCII files. These are text files which when sent to the screen or printer are interpreted as text, unlike the .COM or .EXE files which are binary.

Edlin can also be used to create the source code of various programming languages, such as Fortran and C. In such cases, remember to give the file the appropriate extension, which for the two languages mentioned, are **.for** and **.c**, respectively. However, if you intend to write large programs which might require extensive editing, you might be better off using a full screen editor or your word processor, provided it can save files in ASCII format.

To invoke **Edlin**, the MS-DOS System disc or a disc that contains it must be in one drive, and the file you want to create or edit must be specified. Thus, typing the command:

```
C:\>Edlin test.txt
```

expects to find both **Edlin** and the fictitious file **test.txt** on the disc in the logged drive (in this case C:), while typing

```
C:\>Edlin A:test.txt
```

expects to find **Edlin** on the disc in the logged drive and the file **test.txt** on the disc in the A: drive.

If the file does not exist on the specified disc, then **Edlin** responds with

```
New File
*_
```

and waits for further commands, while if the file already exists, then **Edlin** loads the file into RAM and responds with

```
End of input file
*_
```

Note the '*' prompt which is characteristic of **Edlin**.

Let us now create a text file, called **test.txt**, which we will use to demonstrate the power of **Edlin**. To start, type at the MS-DOS prompt

```
C:\>Edlin test.txt
```

which should cause **Edlin** to respond with

```
New File
*_
```

if that file does not exist on your disc. If it does exist and you do not want to spoil its contents, then type **q** (for quit) and press the <Enter> key.

The Insert Command on a New File

To insert lines of text, use the command **i** (for insert) at the prompt. In the case of a new file, as no lines of text exist in the file, type 1i and then type in the short text given below.

```
*1i
        1:*first line of text
        2:*second line of text
        3:*^C
*_
```

After typing 1i at the prompt, **Edlin** responds by giving a new line number (in this case 1:) with an asterisk after it to indicate that this is the current line. At this point we type 'first line of text'. On pressing the <Enter> key, **Edlin** gives us an additional line number, now 2:*, into which we type 'second line of text'. Again, on pressing <Enter>, we are offered a further line number, and so on. To end the insertion mode, type **Ctrl+C**. The character **^C** is the two-key depression **Ctrl+C** (hold the key marked **Ctrl** down and press the **C** key).

The List Command

To see what text is in the file, type **l** (for list) at the prompt, as follows:

```
*l
        1: first line of text
        2:*second line of text
*_
```

The line numbers are inserted by **Edlin** so that you can refer to the line you want to edit. The '*' in line 2 indicates that this line was the last to be edited or inserted when **Edlin** was used last.

Note that now there is only one current line. Should the file you are listing be very long, listing in this manner causes the current line to appear in the middle of the listing.

To list specific lines, use the l command with line numbers. For example,

```
*5,151
```

will list lines from 5 to 15 inclusive. Note the syntax of the command which is: "From line number to line number Command". There must be no comma between the second line number and the command letter.

The Edit Mode
To change the current line, type the new line number and press <Enter>. This puts you in edit mode and will cause the line whose number you typed to be displayed. Pressing <Enter> again, confirms that you are happy with the contents of that line, otherwise you can either press the right cursor key to reveal each letter of that line, or re-type the entire line, making any necessary changes. In our case, we want to change line 2 to

```
second line of text, edited
```

so enter the edit mode and change the line appropriately. This is best done by using the right arrow cursor key to reveal the whole of the existing line and then typing the extra information at the end of it. The <Ins> and <Del> keys can also be used to edit the text.

The Insert Command on an Existing File
To insert lines of text, use the command i (for insert) at the prompt. However, be warned. Using i on its own will insert the new line before the current line (the one with the * after the line number). To insert lines at any other point, give the line number before the command.

In our case, we would like to insert two additional lines after the existing two. To do this, type

```
*3i
        3:*third line of text
        4:*fourth line of text
        5:*^C
*_
```

21

Again, insertion mode is terminated in line 5: by pressing **Ctrl+C**. If we now list the contents of the file, we get:

```
*l
        1: first line of text
        2: second line of text, edited
        3: third line of text
        4:*fourth line of text
*_
```

The last line to be inserted becomes the current line.

The Delete Command

To delete unwanted lines of text, use the **d** command (for delete) at the prompt. However, if you use the **d** command without any number associated with it, you will delete the current line (the one with the asterisk). Therefore, if you want to delete line 13, say, type

```
*13d
```

or if you want to delete a group of lines, type

```
*13,15d
```

which is translated as 'lines 13 to 15 to be deleted'.

The Move & Copy Commands

To move or copy text, use the **m** or **c** commands (for move or copy). These commands must be preceded by three numbers, as follows:

```
*13,15,8m
```

which is interpreted as 'lines 13 to 15 to be moved to a position before line 8'.

Similarly, the **c** command will copy a block and insert it before the given line. To move or copy a single line, the first two numbers in the command will have to be the same. After moving or copying lines, always use the list command to force re-numbering of the file's contents.

The Search Command

To search for the occurrence of a word or a specified number of characters in a file you have created using **Edlin**, use the search command. Just as in the list and delete commands, a line range is first specified, followed by the **s** (for search) command. Thus, typing

```
*1,4s edited
```

evokes the response

```
        2: second line of text, edited
   *_
```

which displays the line containing the word 'edited'.

Note that the space between the command **s** and the word 'edited' becomes part of the search string. Had we been searching for the characters 'con' within the word 'second', we would have had to omit the space between the command s and the string 'con'.

The search command finds only the first occurrence of the specified string. To continue the search for further occurrences of the same string, simply type **s** again. Thus, typing

```
*1,4sir
        1: first line of text
*s
        3: third line of text
   *_
```

causes **Edlin** to first find the string 'ir' in the word 'first' of line 1:, then by typing **s** again, it forces **Edlin** to find the same string 'ir' in the word 'third' of line 3:.

The Search & Replace Command
This command is similar to the search command, except that it requires a replacement string. Thus, typing

```
*1,4r edited^Z re-edited
```

will cause all occurrences of the word 'edited' to be replaced by the word 're-edited' in all the specified lines of text. Here, of course, it only occurs once in line 2: of the text. The character **^Z** is the two-key depression **Ctrl+Z** (hold the key marked **Ctrl** down and press the **Z** key), which acts as a delimiter between the two strings. Again note that the space in front of both words becomes part of both the searching and the replacing strings.

The Transfer Command
This command transfers the contents of a file into the file currently being edited. The format of the command is:

[n] T *filespec*

where

n   specifies the line number where the new data is to be inserted. The data is inserted before the specified line. If the line number is omitted, then the current line is used.

filespec specifies the file that you want to insert the contents of into the current file in memory.

Exiting Edlin
To end the current session and exit **Edlin** at any point, type

*e

which saves a new file under the chosen filename.

However, if the filename already existed on disc prior to using **Edlin**, ending **Edlin** has the following effect:

First the name of the old file on the disc is given the extension **.bak**, then the new file you have created by editing the old one is saved with the original extension. In this way you can make mistakes without disastrous effects since the system makes a back-up file of the original. If need be, you could delete the **.txt** file and then rename the back-up file (**.bak**) to its original name and extension.

Note that **Edlin** is disciplined not to allow editing of back-up files so, should you want to start using **Edlin** to edit the contents of a **.bak** file, you must first rename it, by giving it a different extension, before proceeding.

If, on the other hand, you realised that too many mistakes were made during editing, you could use the **q** command to quit, as follows:

*q

instead of using the **e** command as discussed above. Doing this causes **Edlin** to ask you whether you want to abort. Typing **y** (for yes), leaves the name and contents of the original file on disc unaltered.

4. BATCH FILES

A batch file is a text file that, in its simplest form, consists of a list of DOS commands. It must have a name ending with the extension **.bat** (such as **list.bat**). The commands in such a file can be executed by simply typing the file name from the DOS prompt (for example, by typing **list** in the above case). A small amount of time creating batch files can save hours of repetitive typing.

To help you in setting up and maintaining your system's hard disc, you will need to create a few batch files and locate them in a special subdirectory, which you might call \BATCH. Do not forget that to make these batch files always available, you must change the PATH command in the **autoexec.bat** file to include the \BATCH subdirectory.

Simple Batch Files

Let us assume that you need to know the exact name of a DOS command that you have forgotten, and that all your DOS files are stored in the subdirectory \DOS. This can be achieved by creating a batch file to display the contents of the DOS subdirectory, whenever the word **dos** is typed. An example of such a batch file (which we will call **dos.bat**), is:

```
@ECHO OFF
CD \DOS
DIR/P
CD \
```

In the second line, the directory is changed to that of \DOS and the third line causes the contents of the \DOS subdirectory to be displayed using the paging (/P) option. Finally, the fourth line returns the system back to the root directory. Thus, typing **dos**, displays the \DOS subdirectory on the screen. Once you have found the external DOS command you were looking for, typing its name will invoke the command, provided, of course, the \DOS subdirectory is also included in the PATH.

Further, let us assume our system has several different versions of the BASIC programming language all stored in the subdirectory \BASIC, and that we want to be able to access each direct from the root directory. However, we can not include the \BASIC subdirectory in the PATH command within the

autoexec.bat file, as we must be able to specify which version of the Basic language is required. For example, two such versions were included in the IBM PC-DOS System disc (BASIC and BASICA; A for advanced), while GWBASIC (which is the implementation of the language for use with the compatibles) was included with pre-DOS 5 versions of the operating system. MS-DOS 5 includes a superior version of Basic which is a sub-set of Microsoft's QBasic. Apart from the above versions, you might also have BBCBASIC - a version of BBC-Basic which runs on the IBM and compatible machines.

We can create a rather special batch file, in the \BATCH subdirectory, to access any of these Basic interpreters, provided they are all in the same \BASIC subdirectory, with the following commands in a batch file which we shall call **bas.bat**

```
@ECHO OFF
CD \BASIC
%1
CD \
```

Note the variable %1 in line 3. This can take the name of any of the Basic languages mentioned above, provided the appropriate name is typed after the batch file name, when it is run. For example, typing:

```
BAS QBASIC
```

at the prompt, starts executing the commands within the batch file **bas.bat**, but substituting QBASIC for the %1 variable.

Thus, line 3 causes entry into QBASIC, provided it exists in the BASIC directory. Similarly, typing:

```
BAS GWBASIC
```

causes entry into GWBASIC.

Alternatively, we could use named parameters in batch files which allow definition of replaceable parameters by name instead of by number. To identify named parameters, we use two percent signs, as follows:

```
%BASTYPE%
```

We can use the SET command to define the named parameter. For example, the command:

```
SET BASTYPE=QBASIC
```

replaces the %BASTYPE% parameter by the filename QBASIC. The SET command can be used either before the batch file is run, or it can be included within the batch file itself. Thus, the DOS environment variables can be defined as named parameters in a batch file to allow different environments for different applications.

Special Batch-file Commands
Apart from the DOS commands, there are some specific commands which can only be used for batch-file processing.

Command	Action
CALL	Allows you to call one batch file from within another. The general form of the command is:

CALL filespec

where *filespec* specifies the drive, subdirectory and name of the batch file to be called. This file must have the extension **.bat**, (which must not be included in the file-spec part of the CALL command).

In the case of pre-v3.3 of DOS, the CALL command can only be used as the last statement of the current file to call another batch file. Return to the first batch file is not possible.

In the case of DOS v3.3 and later, the CALL command can be issued from any place within the current batch file to pass control and execute another batch file. On termination of the called batch file, execution control returns to the calling batch file at the command following the CALL command.

Pipes and redirection symbols must not be used with the CALL command. Batch files that require replaceable parameters

27

can be CALLed. The CALL command can be used to call the current batch file, but care must be taken to eventually terminate execution of the batch file.

ECHO

Enables or disables the screen display of MS-DOS commands which are being executed from within a batch file, or displays the message that follows ECHO. To get a blank line on your display use the command:

echo.

To prevent any commands being echoed to the screen while a batch file is running place the following line at the beginning of the file:

@echo off

This only works with v3.3 DOS and later.

FOR

Repeats the specified MS-DOS command for each 'variable' in the specified 'set of files'. The general form of the command is:

FOR %%variable IN (set of files) DO command

where *command* can include any DOS command or a reference to the %%var. For example,

FOR %%X IN (F.OLD F.NEW) DO TYPE %%X

will display F.OLD followed by F.NEW.

GOTO label

Transfers control to the line which contains the specified label. For example,

GOTO end

:end

sends program control to the **:end** label.

28

IF	Allows conditional command execution. The general form of the command is: IF [NOT] condition command where *condition* can be one of EXIST filespec string1==string2 ERRORLEVEL=n Each of these can be made into a negative condition with the use of the NOT after the IF command.
PAUSE	Suspends execution of a batch file.
REM	Used for adding REMarks to a batch file. Lines beginning with REM are ignored.
SHIFT	Allows batch files to use more than 10 replaceable parameters in batch file processing. An example of this is as follows: @echo off :begin TYPE %1 | MORE PAUSE SHIFT IF EXIST %1 GOTO begin If we call this batch file **display.bat**, then we could look at several different files in succession by simply typing: display file1 file2 file3 The SHIFT command causes each to be taken in turn.

Environment Variables:

The system environment is controlled by 'environment variables' which have names and values allocated to them. The SET command can be used to display, change or delete these environment variables. SET typed without parameters displays the current environment.

Some software packages require you to SET environment variables to their specifications if the package is to work correctly. However, since there is a limited amount of space allocated to the environment by DOS, space held by these variables in the environment should be freed when no longer needed. This is achieved by typing SET followed by the environment variable and the = sign.

Environment variables can be used in a batch file to represent the variables' value, provided the environment variable is enclosed in percent signs (i.e. %PATH%).

For example, typing at the command line

```
FOR %N IN (%PATH%) DO ECHO %N
```

will produce the output

```
C:\
C:\DOS
C:\BATCH
C:\UTILS
```

on the screen, provided you have included these directories in the PATH. If you intend to include the above line in a batch file, remember that you need to include two percent signs before N (i.e. %%N) in both occurrences in the FOR statement.

As an example of this, let us write a batch file which will display the contents of the **autoexec.bat** and **config.sys** files on the screen. This could, of course, be achieved by using the **type** command at the prompt and specifying the name of each file individually. To achieve the same thing, use either **Edit** or **Edlin** to create the file **show.bat** in the \BATCH directory, as follows:

```
CLS
FOR %%N IN (\CONFIG.SYS \AUTOEXEC.BAT) DO
TYPE %%N
@ECHO OFF
CD\
```

which, from now on, when you type **show**, will display the following, or something like it, on your screen:

```
C:\>FOR %N IN (\CONFIG.SYS \AUTOEXEC.BAT)
DO TYPE %N
```

```
C:\>TYPE \CONFIG.SYS
FILES = 20
BUFFERS = 30
BREAK ON
COUNTRY=044,437,C:\DOS\COUNTRY.SYS
DEVICE=C:\DOS\ANSI.SYS

C:\>TYPE \AUTOEXEC.BAT
@ECHO OFF
PATH C:\;C:\DOS;C:\BATCH;C:\UTILS
C:\DOS\APPEND \BATCH
MOUSE
C:\DOS\KEYB UK,437,C:\DOS\KEYBOARD.SYS
PROMPT $P$G
SET TEMP=D:\
ECHO HELLO ... This is your PC using
VER
```

The contents of these two files may well differ considerably from those of your system, particularly if you are using MS-DOS 5 on a 386/486 computer with over 1 Mbyte of RAM.

The MORE Command:

The MORE command displays one screen of output at a time. It can best be used with the 'redirection characters' (<, > and >>), as shown in the following batch file. Type this with your text editor and give it the name **addtext.bat**.

```
@ECHO OFF
CLS
IF "%1"=="" GOTO Error
ECHO. Press 'F6' & 'ENTER' to end session
IF NOT EXIST %1 GOTO Newfile
MORE<%1
:Newfile
MORE>>%1
GOTO Quit
:Error
ECHO. This batch file opens a new text
ECHO. file, and lets you add text
ECHO. on the screen, or opens an existing
ECHO. file and appends text to it.
ECHO.
ECHO. To use type: %0 'filename'
:Quit
```

This batch file could be used instead of **Edlin** for creating, or adding text lines to, another batch file. Try it out by typing:

```
addtext
```

from the DOS prompt. Line 3 checks to ensure the name of the file to be worked on is given in the command line. In our case it was not, so the :Error routine (following line 10) is invoked and instructions are output to the screen. Now type:

```
addtext test.txt
```

A blinking cursor should show below an instruction line at the top of the screen. Add some lines to **test.txt** by typing:

```
line 1
line 2
```

Use the <Enter> key at the end of each line, except the last. Save the file and return to the DOS prompt by pressing <F6> followed by <Enter>. To check the contents of the new file type:

```
addtext test.txt
```

The file is displayed on the screen and you can append more lines if you need to. You can try this out on your own. Unfortunately this batch file will not let you edit the contents of a line once you have ENTERed it, but it does give a quick way of working with short batch files.

In **addtext.bat** line 6 uses the '<' redirection character to direct the contents of the file named by the variable %1 through the MORE command, which causes it to display on the screen one page at a time. Command is then passed to line 8 where MORE appends any collected screen information to the file named by %1 with the '>>' redirection character. If a single '>' character had been used the routed text would have overwritten any previous contents of the file.

5. THE ANSI.SYS COMMANDS

Overview of ANSI.SYS Commands

ANSI.SYS display commands can be used to position the cursor on any part of the screen, change the intensity of the displayed characters, change their colour, or clear part or all of the screen. ANSI.SYS keyboard commands can be used to re-define keys. For example, you could re-define the function keys so that when you press one a complete command is issued as if it was typed at the keyboard.

ANSI.SYS commands are also called 'escape sequences' because they all begin with the ESCape character (code 27) followed by a left square bracket ([). Commands can also include a numeric or alphabetic code, and each command ends with a different letter. The general form of the command is written as:

```
ESC[<code><letter>
```

where the <code> is a numeric or string value and the ending <letter> identifies the command and is case sensitive (that is, H has a different meaning to h, the former identifying the command that moves the cursor, while the latter sets the display mode). Sometimes, the <code> value might be more than one number or string, in which case it is separated by semi-colons. For example,

```
ESC[2J
```

clears the screen, while

```
ESC[2;35H
```

moves the cursor to the 2nd row and 35th column.

ANSI.SYS commands cannot be typed directly into the keyboard because on receiving the ESCape code, MS-DOS cancels the command. Instead, a text editor, such as **Edit** or **Edlin**, has to be used to create a file with the ESCape codes inserted in command lines. The ANSI.SYS commands in the file can then be sent to the console with the use of the ECHO command, or the entire contents of the file can be displayed with the use of the **type** command.

These commands, and the way they are inserted into **Edit** or **Edlin**, will be discussed fully now.

The ANSI.SYS Console Commands

The ANSI.SYS commands for controlling the console (display and keyboard) fall into four groups. The first three of these have to do with the control of the display, while the fourth deals with the control of the keyboard. They are:

(a) Cursor control commands,
(b) Erase display commands,
(c) Attribute and mode commands, and
(d) Keyboard control commands.

What follows is a complete summary of all ANSI.SYS console commands appearing under their appropriate category. Each command starts with ESC[(the ESCape character-code 27, followed by a left bracket). The general form of the command is:

```
ESC[<code><letter>
```

where <code> is a string or numeric value (if more than one, they are separated by semi-colons) which identifies the display attribute, display mode, column or row number (or both) to which the cursor is to be moved, the string to be produced when a key is pressed, or the key to be defined. The ending <letter> identifies the command and is case sensitive.

Cursor Control Commands:

===

Cursor Position   ESC[#;#H or ESC[#;#f

Moves the cursor to the specified position. The first # specifies the row (1-25), while the second # specifies the column (1-80) to which the cursor is to be moved. If either the row or column is omitted, their default value, which is 1, is taken.

To omit row, but specify column, the semi-colon must follow the left bracket. If both row and column are omitted then the cursor moves to the home position which is the upper left corner of the screen.

Cursor Up	ESC[#A
	Moves the cursor up without changing column. The value of # specifies the number of rows by which the cursor is to move up. If the cursor is on the first row, the sequence is ignored. The default value is 1.
Cursor Down	ESC[#B
	Moves the cursor down without changing column. The value of # specifies the number of rows by which the cursor is to move down. If the cursor is on the last row, the sequence is ignored. The default value is 1.
Cursor Right	ESC[#C
	Moves the cursor to the right without changing rows. If the cursor is on the last column, the sequence is ignored. The default value is 1.
Cursor Left	ESC[#D
	Moves the cursor to the left without changing rows. If the cursor is on the first column, the sequence is ignored. The default value is 1.
Save Cursor Position	ESC[s
	Saves the current cursor position. The cursor can be moved to this position later with a Restore Cursor Position command.

Restore Cursor Position ESC[u

> Restores the cursor position to the value it had when it was last saved with the Save Cursor Position command.

Cursor Position Report ESC[#;#R

> Reports the current cursor position to the standard input device. The first # specifies the current row, while the second # specifies the current column.

Device Status Report ESC[6n

> When this command is received, the console driver outputs a Cursor Position Report sequence.

Erase Display Commands:

Erase Display ESC[2J

> Erases the screen and moves the cursor to the home position.

Erase Line ESC[K

> Erases all text from the current cursor position to the end of the line.

Attribute and Mode Commands:

Set Attribute ESC[#;...;#m

> Turns on a display attribute. More than one attribute can be specified provided they are separated by semi-colons.

Omitting the value of attribute is equivalent to specifying attribute 0, which turns off all attributes.

Attribute parameter numbers can be any of the following:

Attribute	Colour	Foregrd	Backgrd
0 None	Black	30	40
1 Bold	Red	31	41
4 Underline	Green	32	42
5 Blink	Yellow	33	43
7 Inverse	Blue	34	44
8 Invisible	Magenta	35	45
	Cyan	36	46
	White	37	47

Set Display Mode

ESC[=#h

Changes the screen mode and allows line wrap at the 80th column.

A mode parameter number can be one of the following:

Param	Mode
0	40x25 b&w
1	40x25 colour on
2	80x25 b&w
3	80x25 colour on
4	320x200 graphics, colour on
5	320x200 graphics, b&w
6	640x200 graphics, b&w
7	Turn on wrap at end of line

Reset Display Mode

ESC[=#l

The reset mode parameter numbers are the same as those for the Set Display Mode, except that parameter number 7 resets the wrap at the end of a line mode. The l is a lower case letter L.

Keyboard Control Commands:

==

Define Key   ESC[#;...;#p

Assigns one or more characters to be produced when a specified key is pressed. The first # specifies the key to be defined, provided the key is one of the standard ASCII characters with a number from 1 to 127. If the key is a function key, keypad key or a combination of Shift+, Ctrl+ or Alt+key and some other key, then two numbers are required separated by a semi-colon, the first of which is always 0 and the second taken from the table overleaf.

The last # is the character or characters to be produced when a key is pressed. It can be defined as an ASCII code, an extended key code, a string enclosed in double quotes, or any combination of codes and strings separated by semi-colons.

Example:

ESC[0;68;"dir | sort | more";13p

re-defines the F10 key so that the directory command is first piped to a sort command, then to a more command, followed by a carriage return.

To restore a key to its original meaning, enter a Define Key command sequence that sets the last # equal to the first #.

Example:

ESC[0;68;0;68p

restores F10 to its original meaning.

Extended Key Codes:

The extended key codes used with the ANSI.SYS Define Key command are shown below. Each key can be pressed 'alone', or with the <Shift>, <Ctrl> or <Alt> keys. A long dash is used in the table to indicate that the key cannot be re-defined.

TABLE 2 Extended Codes - Standard ASCII Characters

Key	Alone	Shift+	Ctrl+	Alt+
Tab	9	0;15	–	–
-	45	95	–	0;130
0	48	41	–	0;129
1	49	33	–	0;120
2	50	64	–	0;121
3	51	35	–	0;122
4	52	36	–	0;123
5	53	37	–	0;124
6	54	94	–	0;125
7	55	38	–	0;126
8	56	42	–	0;127
9	57	40	–	0;128
=	61	43	–	0;131
a	97	65	1	0;30
b	98	66	2	0;48
c	99	67	3	0;46
d	100	68	4	0;32
e	101	69	5	0;18
f	102	70	6	0;33
g	103	71	7	0;34
h	104	72	8	0;35
i	105	73	9	0;23
j	106	74	10	0;36
k	107	75	11	0;37
l	108	76	12	0;38
m	109	77	13	0;50
n	110	78	14	0;49
o	111	79	15	0;24
p	112	80	16	0;25
q	113	81	17	0;16
r	114	82	18	0;19

s	115	83	19	0;31
t	116	84	20	0;20
u	117	85	21	0;22
v	118	86	22	0;47
w	119	87	23	0;17
x	120	88	24	0;45
y	121	89	25	0;21
z	122	90	26	0;44

Extended Codes - Function and Numeric-keypad Keys

Key	Alone	Shift+	Ctrl+	Alt+
F1	0;59	0;84	0;94	0;104
F2	0;60	0;85	0;95	0;105
F3	0;61	0;86	0;96	0;106
F4	0;62	0;87	0;97	0;107
F5	0;63	0;88	0;98	0;108
F6	0;64	0;89	0;99	0;109
F7	0;65	0;90	0;100	0;110
F8	0;66	0;91	0;101	0;111
F9	0;67	0;92	0;102	0;112
F10	0;68	0;93	0;103	0;113
Home	0;71	55	0;119	–
CurUp	0;72	56	–	–
PgUp	0;73	57	0;132	–
CurLft	0;75	52	0;115	–
CurRgt	0;77	54	0;116	–
End	0;79	49	0;117	–
CurDn	0;80	50	–	–
PgDn	0;81	51	0;118	–
Ins	0;82	48	–	–
Del	0;83	46	–	–
PrtSc	–	–	0;114	–

Using Edit to Enter ESCape Commands:

The screen editor **Edit** can be used to enter ESCape command
sequences into a file. The **ESC** character (ASCII 27) is entered
by first typing **Ctrl+P**, then press the <Esc> key which causes
the left arrow (←) to appear on the screen. Thus, to enter

```
ESC[2J
```

which is the ESCape sequence for 'clear screen', evoke **Edit** and type the appropriate character sequence, as shown below:

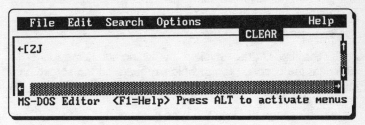

Using Edlin to Enter ESCape Commands:
You can use the **Edlin** line editor to enter ESCape command sequences into a file. The **ESC** character (ASCII 27) is entered by typing **Ctrl+V** (displays as ^V) followed by '['. Thus, to enter

```
ESC[2J
```

which is the ESCape sequence for 'clear screen', evoke **Edlin** and type the appropriate character sequence, as follows:

```
edlin clear
New file
*1i
        1:*^V[[2J
        2:*^C
*e
```

You must type two [[, one as part of the ESCape character and the other as required by the ESC[sequence. It might be a good idea to create this and subsequent example files in a dedicated subdirectory \UTILS.

Note: If you use the **Edlin l** (list) command, you will notice that the ^V[[ESCape sequence has been changed to either [^[(if you are using MS/PC-DOS v3.0 & v3.1), or ^[[(if you are using MS/PC-DOS v3.3 and above).

To send the ESCape sequence to the display and, in this case, clear the screen, we must use the **type** command as follows:

```
type clear
```

41

which clears the screen and causes the prompt to reappear on the second row of the display.

Another way of sending the ESCape sequence to the screen, is from within a batch file using the **echo** command. To do this, we must create a **.bat** file and include the command

```
echo ESC[2J
```

in it. The file is then evoked by typing its name only. To eliminate the second prompt which appears on the screen, you must insert, as a first line in the batch file, an **@echo off** command.

One advantage of using the **type** command to send ESCape sequences to the display, is that it is almost instantaneous. The **echo** method can be very slow, particularly if an elaborate screen is to be built up. For this reason, we will use the "typing" technique to display elaborate screens throughout the rest of this book.

Changing Screen Colours:

As long as ANSI.SYS is loaded in a system it is very easy to change the screen colours displayed by DOS. In the same way as above, generate a text file named **bluescrn** containing the following single line:

```
ESC[0;37;44m
```

If you now use the **type** command as follows:

```
type bluescrn
```

your screen should be set to write in white on a blue background. You may have to clear the screen with the **cls** command to get the full benefit of this.

If you check the table at the top of page 37 you will see why the three numbers in the above ESCape sequence are used. The 0 (zero) sets attributes to "none", the 37 sets the foreground colour to white and the 44 sets blue as the background colour.

We will use this method to control the screen colours when generating our menu system in the next chapter. If you would prefer your system to default to such a blue screen, simply place the **type bluescrn** command in your **autoexec.bat** file, but make sure that the file **bluescrn** is in the \UTILS directory, which should, by now, be on your PATH.

6. DEVELOPING A MENU SYSTEM

We are now in a position to start writing some sample files to produce a simple screen menu system. To do this, use either **Edit, Edlin,** or a proprietary text editor, as explained previously, to enter the ESCape code sequences. Some of the menu files which follow will be much easier to enter with a screen editor, than with **Edlin**.

In all the following examples the ESCape code sequence is shown as {ESC}, with ESC appearing in curly ({ }) brackets to make identification easier. You must, of course, type the code sequence for your editor whenever this appears.

Designing the Main Menu Screen

If you are sitting comfortably, it is time to begin. Type in the 23 line routine shown on the next page and save it as **menumain**. At first glance this looks very complicated, but once you get started you can simplify the job by copying line 3 to form the basis of lines 4-21, then editing the latter lines. Make sure you do this in 'overstrike' mode. Another important thing is to insert the correct number of blank spaces, as shown overleaf.

When finished, exit your editor and from the DOS prompt type, **type menumain.** You should get the following screen layout; if not, you have probably not entered the text correctly.

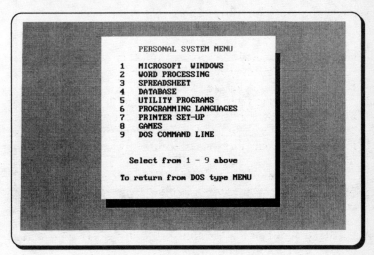

```
[ESC][0;36;44m
[ESC][2J
[ESC][3;23H[ESC][0;30;46m          [ESC][0;31;46mPERSONAL SYSTEM MENU [ESC][m          [ESC][m
[ESC][4;23H[ESC][0;30;46m          [ESC][0;31;46m                     [ESC][0;30;46m
[ESC][5;23H[ESC][0;30;46m                                            [ESC][m
[ESC][6;23H[ESC][0;30;46m     1    MICROSOFT WINDOWS                  [ESC][m
[ESC][7;23H[ESC][0;30;46m     2    WORD PROCESSING                    [ESC][m
[ESC][8;23H[ESC][0;30;46m     3    SPREADSHEET                        [ESC][m
[ESC][9;23H[ESC][0;30;46m     4    DATABASE                           [ESC][m
[ESC][10;23H[ESC][0;30;46m    5    UTILITY PROGRAMS                   [ESC][m
[ESC][11;23H[ESC][0;30;46m    6    PROGRAMMING LANGUAGES              [ESC][m
[ESC][12;23H[ESC][0;30;46m    7    PRINTER SETUP                      [ESC][m
[ESC][13;23H[ESC][0;30;46m    8    GAMES                              [ESC][m
[ESC][14;23H[ESC][0;30;46m    9    DOS COMMAND LINE                   [ESC][m
[ESC][15;23H[ESC][0;30;46m                                            [ESC][m
[ESC][16;23H[ESC][0;30;46m   Select from [ESC][0;31;46m1 - 9 [ESC][0;30;46m above   [ESC][m
[ESC][17;23H[ESC][0;30;46m                                            [ESC][m
[ESC][18;23H[ESC][0;30;46m   To return from DOS type MENU             [ESC][m
[ESC][19;23H[ESC][0;30;46m                                            [ESC][m
[ESC][20;23H[ESC][0;30;46m                                            [ESC][m
[ESC][21;23H[ESC][0;30;46m                            [ESC][m          [ESC][m
[ESC][22;24H
[ESC][0;3;44m
```

44

Note that to get the shadow on the right of the menu display, a space is inserted after each {ESC}[m code of lines 5-22. The position of the code dictates the starting point of the shadow.

Hopefully by now you can see what an improvement our menu will be over the straight DOS prompt. Obviously at the end of the day you will be using the system yourself, on your own machine, so you will need to adapt it to your own set-up.

One look at the screen we have produced should show up two problem areas. The DOS prompt and cursor spoil the bottom left corner of the screen for one. Also at the moment we have no way, with the basic system, of "letting DOS know" which item we have selected from our menu.

Creating Interactive Batch Files

In order to make batch files interactive, we need to create a small program, we will call it **respond.com**, which 'responds' to the keyboard keys most recently pressed. This is a bit similar to the INKEY command in the BASIC computer language that reads a character from the keyboard.

Normally, when a key is pressed, a code representing that key is sent to DOS for translation and subsequent display. However, DOS also stores the value of this code in a part of memory which can be accessed and is normally referred to as the 'errorlevel'. The key codes of both the standard ASCII and extended ASCII characters were discussed earlier and are listed in Tables 1 and 2, respectively.

Because the first number of the two-number value representing the extended key codes is always 0, DOS sets errorlevel to the second number. This, inevitably produces some duplication between standard and extended key codes (for example, the numeric key 0, Alt-b and Shift-Ins all set errorlevel to 48), but we can put up with it because the keys responsible are unrelated.

We will create **respond.com** using **Debug**, but don't get worried no programming knowledge will be required. If you do want to get more involved with **Debug** we have included a short crash course in Appendix A.

Creating a DEBUG Script File:

The easiest way to use **Debug** is to create a text file which contains all the commands for **Debug** to process. This is usually called a script file. Once it has been created DEBUG can be started with the contents of the script file directed to it, with the "<" redirection character.

To create **respond.com**, use **Edlin** to create its script file as follows:

```
edlin respond.scr

    1:*a   0100
    2:*    mov AH,07
    3:*    int 21
    4:*    cmp AL,00
    5:*    jnz 010C
    6:*    mov AH,07
    7:*    int 21
    8:*    mov AH,4C
    9:*    int 21
   10:*
   11:*r  cx
   12:*10
   13:*n respond.com
   14:*w
   15:*q
```

Make sure you type the above with no mistakes. Particularly make sure you do not forget the q in line 15. Without this, **Debug** will hang the system when it is invoked. You can use your text editor to produce the script file if you prefer, in which case do not type the line numbers, colons or asterisks. Make sure you leave line 10 as a blank. Now, invoke **Debug** by typing:

```
debug < respond.scr
```

which will create **respond.com,** the desired program and save it in the \UTILS directory. We will test **respond.com** a little later, but in the meantime will use **Debug** to generate two cursor control programs.

Controlling the Cursor

We can improve the appearance of the previously written menu screen by incorporating two assembly language programs which control the cursor. The first program is designed to turn the cursor off, so that it does not appear in unwanted areas on the screen, while the second is designed to turn it back on again.

Now use **Edlin** to first write the script file **nocurs.scr**, to turn the cursor off, with the following contents:

```
1:* a 0100
2:*    mov AH,01
3:*    mov CH,20
4:*    int 10
5:*    int 20
6:*
7:* r cx
8:* 08
9:* n nocurs.com
10:* w
11:* q
```

then write the script file **normcurs.scr**, to turn the cursor on, with the following contents:

```
1:* a 0100
2:*    mov AH,0F
3:*    int 10
4:*    cmp AL,07
5:*    jz  010D
6:*    mov CX,0607
7:*    jmp 0110
8:*    mov CX,0B0C
9:*    mov AH,01
11:*   int 10
12:*   int 20
13:*
14:* r cx
15:* 16
16:* n normcurs.com
17:* w
18:* q
```

Now, use **Debug** with its input redirected to the script file **nocurs.scr**, to create the **nocurs.com** program, as follows:

```
debug < nocurs.scr
```

followed by the reactivation of **Debug** with its input redirected to the script file **normcurs.scr** to create the **normcurs.com** program.

Both these programs (as indeed all the programs we will create using **Debug**) can be used by themselves, not just in the following batch files. Thus typing **nocurs** will make the cursor disappear from the screen, while typing **normcurs** makes it reappear.

The Menu Batch File

We have now created all the basic components for our menu system. Make sure the following files are present in your \UTILS directory - **menumain**, **bluescrn**, **respond.com**, **nocurs.com** and **normcurs.com**. All we need now is a means of linking these together and controlling the menu system. To do this we will generate a batch file called **menu.bat**. In its initial form this will be used to test that our components and logic are satisfactory. Use your screen editor to enter **menu.bat**, as follows:

```
@ECHO OFF
CLS

:again
C:
CD \UTILS
TYPE menumain
nocurs

:getkey
respond
IF ERRORLEVEL 58 GOTO getkey
IF ERRORLEVEL 57 GOTO dos
IF ERRORLEVEL 56 GOTO games
IF ERRORLEVEL 55 GOTO printer
IF ERRORLEVEL 54 GOTO proglang
IF ERRORLEVEL 53 GOTO utilities
IF ERRORLEVEL 52 GOTO database
IF ERRORLEVEL 51 GOTO spreadsheet
IF ERRORLEVEL 50 GOTO wp
IF ERRORLEVEL 49 GOTO windows
IF NOT ERRORLEVEL 49 GOTO getkey

:dos
CLS
TYPE bluescrn
GOTO quit
```

cont...

```
:games
normcurs
CLS
ECHO. Games
PAUSE
GOTO again

:printer
normcurs
CLS
ECHO. Printer
PAUSE
GOTO again

:proglang
normcurs
CLS
ECHO. Programming languages
PAUSE
GOTO again

:database
normcurs
CLS
ECHO. Database
PAUSE
GOTO again

:utilities
normcurs
CLS
ECHO. Utility routines
PAUSE
GOTO again

:spreadsheet
normcurs
CLS
ECHO. Spreadsheet
PAUSE
GOTO again

:wp
normcurs
CLS
ECHO. Word processor
PAUSE
```

cont...

```
GOTO again

:windows
win
GOTO again

:quit
ECHO.To return to the MENU SYSTEM type MENU
C:
CD \
normcurs
```

Now, when you run **menu.bat,** by typing **menu,** your main screen menu should display without a flashing cursor.

Menu.bat has been designed to be as modular as possible; this helps to make its operation easier to understand and should facilitate any future changes to the file which may be required when you customise the menu to your system. Each module has a label and is accessed with the GOTO command. The :**again** module makes the C:\UTILS directory current (not strictly necessary if it is on the path), types the main menu on the screen and removes the cursor. Control then passes to :**getkey** which uses the **respond** program to check which key is pressed and stores it as 'errorlevel' if it is a number between 1 and 9. The next 11 lines are the core of the system, they check which key was pressed and direct the next action accordingly. The line

```
IF ERRORLEVEL 58 GOTO getkey
```

checks whether the ASCII code of the key pressed is equal to or greater than 58. (All keys with an ASCII code greater than that of the digit 9). If one of these was pressed the getkey routine is repeated. Succeeding lines check for code 57 (the digit 9), code 56 (the digit 8)... down to code 49 (the digit 1) and route control to the required subroutine with the GOTO command. The last line of :**getkey** ensures that no other codes will be acted upon.

Because the IF command checks that ERRORLEVEL is equal to or greater than the number stated, the routine must start the testing sequence with the highest code numbers and work down to the lowest (58 down to 49, in our example).

The other labelled routines are self explanatory. Any useful menu system must give the user a way of 'escaping' from it, especially while it is being developed. In our case the DOS COMMAND LINE option provides this. It produces a cleared blue screen with instructions on how to get back to the menu, followed by the DOS prompt. The only other menu option that does anything useful at the moment is the Windows option. This of course assumes that you have Microsoft Windows installed in the standard way on your system, in which case just typing **WIN** from the DOS prompt will start the program up. The **:windows** routine does just this and is followed by the **GOTO again** statement to return command to the main menu when the Windows program is closed. All the other routines in **menu.bat** are set up to test that the interactive section of the system works correctly. Once you have tested them you can change the test routine to one that is more meaningful for your system.

As an example, let's assume you have the Lotus 1-2-3 spreadsheet installed on your system in the C:\LOTUS directory and to start the program requires the command **123** to be given from that directory. To implement this in our menu you would need to change the **:spreadsheet** routine to the following:

```
normcurs
CLS
C:
CD \LOTUS
123
GOTO again
```

The **normcurs** command is to ensure that the cursor is available when the menu is not being displayed. Of course if you had more than one spreadsheet on your computer the above routine would not be satisfactory; in that case you could easily create a second menu screen to facilitate the choice between them. This procedure will be demonstrated when we build the PRINTER SET-UP routine later.

If you have worked through to this section of the chapter you should have no problems customising some of the other menu options for your system.

Controlling your Printer

In our experience more people have trouble setting up and controlling their printer than any other piece of computer hardware. When you use a proprietary software package, such as a word processor, as long as it is installed correctly, it will take over control of the printer. If, however, you want to print text files from the DOS environment, you may find that a little help comes in useful. The two most popular 'types of printers' are the Epson compatible dot matrix and the Hewlett-Packard (HP) compatible laser. Nearly all modern printers should be able to emulate one of these types. With both of them you can use ANSI.SYS ESCape codes to send control instructions to the printer. Detailed control codes for both these types of printer are given in Appendix C. Our menu system will include an example of some of the more useful commands for each printer type, but you can change these if you so wish.

The ESC character code 27 is a particularly important one for printers. It has the special meaning that the next character specifies a printer command, not something to be printed. Sending the character "4" to an Epson compatible printer will cause it to print the number 4, but sending ESC4 will cause the printer to start printing in italic mode.

The way we will send codes to the printer is by redirecting ECHO commands. For example the above would be:

```
ECHO {ESC}4> PRN
```

These could be typed in from the keyboard, or more easily, included in a batch file.

An EPSON Printer Menu:
Load the file **menumain** into your text editor, edit it using 'overstrike', to the text shown below, and save it as **menuepsn**.

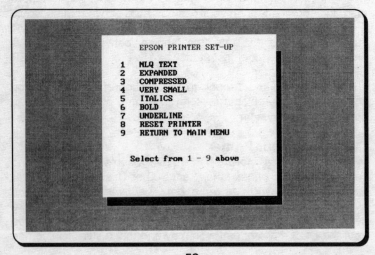

```
                    EPSON PRINTER SET-UP

        1    NLQ TEXT
        2    EXPANDED
        3    COMPRESSED
        4    VERY SMALL
        5    ITALICS
        6    BOLD
        7    UNDERLINE
        8    RESET PRINTER
        9    RETURN TO MAIN MENU


           Select from 1 - 9 above
```

As you can see, once you have made up one full menu screen, it is a very easy matter to adapt it, by simply editing the text shown in the box. If you prefer, you could of course experiment with different box colours, sizes and shading. Make sure your new menu screen is correct with the **type menuepsn** command.

When you are happy with it enter the following file with your editor and call it **prnepson.bat**. You would probably find it much easier to adapt the file **menu.bat**, as they are quite similar.

Note: When entering the ESCape code sequences make sure that you do not leave any spaces, especially in front of the redirection character '>'. The command for compressed text does not have an ESCape in it, but the character '¤'. This is often written as <Alt+15>. With both the DOS and Norton editors it is obtained by typing **Ctrl+P**, then 15 typed from the numeric key pad on the right of the keyboard, while the **Alt** key is depressed. Depending on your editor this may show as either '¤', or as '^O'.

```
@ECHO OFF
CLS

:again
C:
CD \UTILS
TYPE menuepsn
nocurs

:getkey
respond
IF ERRORLEVEL 58 GOTO getkey
IF ERRORLEVEL 57 GOTO quit
IF ERRORLEVEL 56 GOTO reset
IF ERRORLEVEL 55 GOTO underline
IF ERRORLEVEL 54 GOTO bold
IF ERRORLEVEL 53 GOTO italics
IF ERRORLEVEL 52 GOTO vsmall
IF ERRORLEVEL 51 GOTO compressed
IF ERRORLEVEL 50 GOTO expanded
IF ERRORLEVEL 49 GOTO nlq
IF NOT ERRORLEVEL 49 GOTO getkey

:nlq
ECHO {ESC}x1> PRN
GOTO getkey
```

53

```
:expanded
ECHO {ESC}W1> PRN
GOTO getkey

:compressed
ECHO ¤> PRN
GOTO getkey

:vsmall
ECHO ¤{ESC}S0{ESC}3¤> PRN
GOTO getkey

:italics
ECHO {ESC}4> PRN
GOTO getkey

:bold
ECHO {ESC}E> PRN
GOTO getkey

:underline
ECHO {ESC}-1> PRN
GOTO getkey

:reset
ECHO {ESC}@> PRN
GOTO getkey

:quit
menu
```

Before trying out this printer menu link it into the main menu by altering the **:printer** routine of the file **menu.bat** to the following:

```
:printer
prnepson
GOTO again
```

You should now have a working printer set-up menu which operates as a sub-menu of the main one. Try it out by typing **menu** and selecting option 7. If your printer is Epson compatible, you should be able to force it to print compressed text, when next used, by selecting 3 and then 9 to return to the main menu. Return to the DOS prompt and type:

```
COPY prnepson.bat LPT1
```

If all is well you should get a print-out that can hold up to 132 characters per normal 80 character line.

If that is not small enough, the 'very small' option should print text small enough to almost need a magnifying glass to read! This option does three things - turns compressed print on, starts superscript and sets the line spacing to $^{15}/_{216}$ inch. The **LPT1** in the above command assumes your printer is connected to the parallel port of your computer.

An HP (PCL) Printer Menu:
If you use a laser printer which can use the Hewlett-Packard printer control language (PCL), the following sub menu will be of more use. Load the file **menumain** into your text editor, edit it, using 'overstrike', to the text shown below, and save it as **menuhp.**

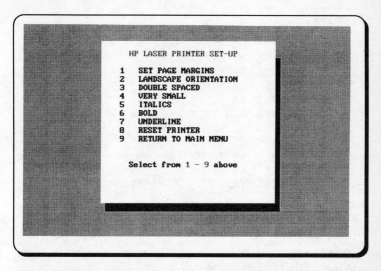

As you can see, once you have made up one full menu screen, it is an easy matter to adapt it, by simply editing the text shown in the box. If you prefer, you could of course experiment with different box colours, sizes and shading. Make sure your new menu screen is correct with the **type menuhp** command.

When you are happy with it, enter the following file with your editor and call it **prnhp.bat**. You would probably find it much easier to adapt the file **menu.bat**, as the two files have much in common.

Note: When entering the ESCape code sequences make sure that you do not leave any spaces, especially in front of the redirection character '>'.

In several of the ESCape sequences below the '&' character is followed by 'l' which is a lower case 'L', so do not confuse it with the digit '1' when you enter text.

```
@ECHO OFF
CLS

:again
C:
CD \UTILS
TYPE menuhp
nocurs

:getkey
respond
IF ERRORLEVEL 58 GOTO getkey
IF ERRORLEVEL 57 GOTO quit
IF ERRORLEVEL 56 GOTO reset
IF ERRORLEVEL 55 GOTO underline
IF ERRORLEVEL 54 GOTO bold
IF ERRORLEVEL 53 GOTO italics
IF ERRORLEVEL 52 GOTO vsmall
IF ERRORLEVEL 51 GOTO double
IF ERRORLEVEL 50 GOTO landscape
IF ERRORLEVEL 49 GOTO margins
IF NOT ERRORLEVEL 49 GOTO getkey

:margins
ECHO {ESC}&a5L{ESC}&15E> PRN
GOTO getkey

:landscape
ECHO {ESC}&l1O> PRN
GOTO getkey

:double
ECHO {ESC}&l3D> PRN
GOTO getkey

:vsmall
ECHO {ESC}(s16.66H{ESC}&14C> PRN
GOTO getkey
```

cont...

```
:italics
ECHO {ESC}(s1S> PRN
GOTO getkey

:bold
ECHO {ESC}(s3B> PRN
GOTO getkey

:underline
ECHO {ESC}&d0D> PRN
GOTO getkey

:reset
ECHO {ESC}E> PRN
GOTO getkey

:quit
menu
```

Before trying out this printer menu link it into the main menu by altering the **:printer** routine of the file **menu.bat** to the following:

```
:printer
prnhp
GOTO again
```

You should now have a working printer set-up menu which operates as a sub-menu of the main one. Try it out by typing **menu** and selecting option 7. If your printer is HP laser compatible, you should be able to set it to print with landscape orientation when next used (prints across the page instead of down the page), by selecting 2 and then 9 to return to the main menu. Return to the DOS prompt and type:

```
COPY menumain LPT1
```

If all is well, you should get a print out across the page. If the print is not small enough, you could try the 'small print' option. The **LPT1** in the above command assumes your laser printer is connected to the parallel port of your computer.

A Laser Printer Batch File:
While we are on the subject of controlling HP laser printers, you may find the following batch file useful for printing the odd text file. Try it out by typing it with your editor and naming it **hpprint.bat.**

```
@ECHO OFF
REM  Print control of HP LaserJet

IF "%1"=="" GOTO error
REM Set orientation - landscape or portrait
REM  1 = landscape, 0 = portrait
ECHO {ESC}&l1O> PRN

REM  Set top margin to 5 lines
ECHO {ESC}&l5E> PRN

REM  Set left column to 3 columns
ECHO {ESC}&a3L> PRN

COPY %1 lpt1

REM  Resets printer and ejects page
ECHO {ESC}E> PRN
GOTO QUIT

:error
ECHO.HP LaserJet print control
ECHO.Needs a file name to print
ECHO.
ECHO.Type  HPPRINT filename
ECHO.

:quit
```

This batch file expects you to enter **hpprint <filename>** from the DOS prompt, where <filename> is the name of the file you want to print.

Several of the control lines in it are very easy to modify, so that you can customise it to your needs. Line 6 controls whether your printing is landscape or portrait orientated. The penultimate character in the ESCape sequence **{ESC}&l1O**, is '1' which sets the printer to landscape mode. A zero character ('0') here, would force portrait orientation.

The digit '5' in line 8 sets the top paper margin to 5 lines, while in line 10 the digit '3' sets the left paper margin to 3 columns of print. By changing these two numbers in the batch file you can set the margins to wherever you want them to be.

Sample Utilities Menu

To complete the menu system layout we will build a utilities sub-menu containing some routines you may find useful for your system. These are only examples and you can, of course, build up your own set of routines. In fact, some of the batch files developed in the next chapter could be included.

Load the file **menumain** into your text editor and, as before, edit the menu text to the following using overstrike mode. Save the file as **menutils**.

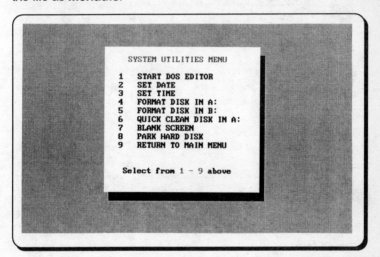

```
SYSTEM UTILITIES MENU

1    START DOS EDITOR
2    SET DATE
3    SET TIME
4    FORMAT DISK IN A:
5    FORMAT DISK IN B:
6    QUICK CLEAN DISK IN A:
7    BLANK SCREEN
8    PARK HARD DISK
9    RETURN TO MAIN MENU

Select from 1 - 9 above
```

Some of these routines are simple commands which could be implemented at the DOS prompt, but once you get used to using the menu system you will probably prefer to work from it for as much of the time as possible.

Adapt one of the previous menu batch files to the following, with your text editor, and save it as **utils.bat**:

```
@ECHO OFF
CLS

:again
C:
CD \UTILS
TYPE menutils
nocurs                              cont...
```

```
:getkey
respond
IF ERRORLEVEL 58 GOTO getkey
IF ERRORLEVEL 57 GOTO quit
IF ERRORLEVEL 56 GOTO park
IF ERRORLEVEL 55 GOTO screensave
IF ERRORLEVEL 54 GOTO cleanA
IF ERRORLEVEL 53 GOTO formatB
IF ERRORLEVEL 52 GOTO formatA
IF ERRORLEVEL 51 GOTO setime
IF ERRORLEVEL 50 GOTO setdate
IF ERRORLEVEL 49 GOTO editor
IF NOT ERRORLEVEL 49 GOTO getkey

:editor
CLS
normcurs
C:
CD \DOS
Edit
GOTO again

:setdate
normcurs
CLS
DATE
GOTO again

:setime
normcurs
CLS
TIME
GOTO again

:formatA
normcurs
CLS
FORMAT A: /F:1.44mb
GOTO again

:formatB
normcurs
CLS
FORMAT B: /F:1.2mb
GOTO again
```

cont...

```
:cleanA
normcurs
CLS
ECHO.WARNING
ECHO.THIS WILL DESTROY ALL THE
ECHO.FILES AND DIRECTORIES ON THE
ECHO.DISC IN DRIVE A:
ECHO.
ECHO.PRESS THE F1 KEY TO ABORT
ECHO.ANY OTHER KEY TO CONTINUE
respond
IF ERRORLEVEL 59 IF NOT ERRORLEVEL 60 GOTO again
ECHO Y|RECOVER A: > NUL
ECHO Y|DEL A:*.* > NUL
GOTO again

:screensave
ECHO {ESC}[0;30;30m
CLS
PAUSE>NUL
GOTO again

:park
CLS
PARK
GOTO again

:quit
menu
```

Link this utilities sub-menu into the main menu by simply altering the **:utilities** routine of the file **menu.bat** to the following:

```
:utilities
utils
GOTO again
```

The **:editor** routine simply calls the Microsoft editor **Edit** which is usually kept in the C:\DOS directory. The **:setdate** and **:setime** routines allow you to adjust the date and time as used by your system. If you do not keep these correct, your files will be stamped incorrectly whenever they are saved.

Formatting Floppy Discs:

The next two routines allow you to format floppy discs in your A: and B: drives. The assumption has been made that your A: drive is a 3.5-inch, high density drive, capable of using 1.44MB discs and that B: is a 5.25-inch drive capable of using 1.2MB discs. This obviously will not apply to everyone. If your system is different, change the fourth line of the **:format** routines to whichever of the following are applicable.

Using a 1.44MB, double-sided, quadruple density, 3.5-inch drive:

```
FORMAT n: /F:1.44mb
```

Using a 1.2MB, double-sided, quadruple density, 5.25-inch drive:

```
FORMAT n: /F:1.2mb
```

Using a 720KB, double-sided, double density, 3.5-inch drive:

```
FORMAT n: /F:720kb
```

Using a 360KB, double-sided, double density, 5.25-inch drive:

```
FORMAT n: /F:360kb
```

To format a 360KB disc in a 5.25-inch high density drive:

```
FORMAT n: /4
```

The last command should produce formatted discs which are usable in your own drive but they may well not work in all other disc drives. You may need to experiment here. In all of the above, the 'n' should be replaced by the drive letter being used, either 'a' or 'b'.

Needless to say, you should be careful when using the FORMAT command. If by mistake you specify your hard disc drive, instead of a floppy disc drive, the results could be catastrophic.

Cleaning a Floppy Disc:

The routine in **:cleanA** clears all the files and subdirectories from the disc in the A: drive, leaving an empty disc. This uses the RECOVER command which, without a filename as a parameter, assigns all the files on the disc a new filename in the root directory. The existing files and subdirectories are simply discarded - see 'warning' on the next page.

WARNING: If you specify a hard disc drive in this routine you will lose all the contents of that drive, so be very careful how you type in the text.

The first few lines of **:cleanA**, produce a screen warning and the option to abort the procedure. The line

```
IF ERRORLEVEL 59 IF NOT ERRORLEVEL 60 GOTO again
```

checks what key has been pressed and stored by the **respond** command. If the **F1** key was pressed (ASCII 59), command is transferred to **:again** and the routine is aborted. Any other key will be ignored by this line. This demonstrates a useful procedure for checking for individual key strokes in batch files. The first part of the **IF** statement is satisfied if the ASCII code of the key pressed is 59 or higher. The second part (IF NOT ERRORLEVEL 60), excludes keys with codes of 60 or above, thus leaving only 59 (the **F1** key), to satisfy the two **IF** tests.

The next line

```
ECHO Y|RECOVER A: > NUL
```

echoes a 'Y' character to the **RECOVER** command through a pipe, the '|' character. The 'Y' pre-answers a question that the RECOVER utility asks and prevents the operation from stopping. The '> **NUL**' redirects the output from RECOVER to the NUL device, which prevents it showing on the screen. It simply goes nowhere.

The next line echoes a 'Y' to the **DEL A:*.*** command, which then deletes all the files created on the disc by the previous line, without stopping and 'asking' if this is OK. Again, the written output is redirected to NUL to keep the screen clean.

As the DOS command RECOVER is a potentially dangerous utility, if you have version 5 of DOS you could use a quick format procedure to clear your floppy discs. The command:

```
FORMAT A: /Q
```

could replace the middle 11 lines of the **:cleanA** routine. This command only works on previously formatted discs. It checks the disc's existing format-type and carries out a rapid reformat.

Even if you use this quick format procedure, some of the 'tricks' included in the original batch file above, could be usefully employed in your future batch files.

A Simple Screensave Utility:

Some people worry that leaving their computer switched on for any length of time with the same screen display may cause damage to the monitor screen. To obviate this, the **:screensave** routine blanks out the screen when selected, until any key is pressed, when the menu returns for use.
The line:

```
ECHO {ESC}[0;30;30m
```

sets the screen to black background and foreground, the **CLS** command following, implements this and blanks the screen. **PAUSE>NUL** halts the system until a key is pressed, the usual screen output from this command being redirected to the NUL device for neatness.

Parking your Hard Disc:

The **:park** routine assumes you have a utility that parks your hard disc and that it is stored on the system path, most likely in the C:\DOS directory. It is good practice to park a hard disc-drive when the computer is switched off to avoid the possibility of damage if the unit is bumped or moved. The parking action moves the drive heads to a section of the disc not used to store data.

Implementing your Own Menu System

You should now have all the tools to hand to build yourself a professional looking menu system for your PC. If necessary, you can nest as many sub-menus as you like, to give you an enormous amount of flexibility. Do not forget though, to always build in a route to let you move back out of the system, to the main menu and then to DOS.

Automating your Menu System:

Once you are happy with your own menu system and it operates with no problems, you can invoke it automatically every time your computer starts up. To do this simply add the command **menu** to the end of your **autoexec.bat** file using your text editor.

7. OTHER SYSTEM BATCH FILES

This chapter contains an assortment of other batch files and routines which we have found useful over a period of time. It is suggested that you try them out for yourself. We think that it is only by using existing batch files and puzzling out how they work that you can master the art of handling the DOS command language.

All your batch files should be placed in one dedicated directory, usually C:\BATCH, which must be listed on the PATH command of your **autoexec.bat** file.

File Management

Even without expensive utilities you can easily locate a file anywhere on a drive, however complicated the directory structure. Type in the file **findfile.bat**, as follows:

```
@ECHO OFF
CLS
CD \
IF "%1"=="" GOTO message
ATTRIB %1 /S
GOTO quit

:message
ECHO.Input the name of the file
ECHO.you want to locate.
ECHO.
ECHO.For example FINDFILE filename.ext

:quit
```

Try it out by typing **findfile <filename.ext>** at the prompt. If the file searched for exists on the drive, its full path, as well as a list of its attributes, (A: Archive, R: Read-only, H: Hidden, S: System) will be displayed before the prompt is restored.

Do not forget the '/S' after the **ATTRIB** statement, as this forces the search to include all subdirectories on the drive.

The wild card characters '*' and '?' can be used in the filename to extend the power of the search. For example,

.	would list all files on the drive
*.tmp	would list all files with the extension .tmp
*.t??	would list all files with an extension starting with a 't'.

Moving Files

DOS does not have a command to move a file, or files, from one location to another. You have to first COPY them, then DELete or ERASE the originals. It is easy to write a batch file to carry out these operations, but you must be careful to check that the copied file(s) actually exist in the new location before the original(s) are deleted. If, for example, you specify an incorrect path to the destination location, the file(s) would not be copied but the original(s) would be lost. The following file, call it **move.bat**, checks that the copy operation has been successful before carrying out the deletion.

```
REM MOVE.BAT
@ECHO OFF
CLS
IF "%2"=="" GOTO message
GOTO move

:message
ECHO.^G You must specify what to move
ECHO. and where to move it!
ECHO.
ECHO. For example move *.txt a:\*.txt
ECHO.
GOTO quit

:move
COPY %1 %2 > NUL
IF NOT EXIST %2 GOTO fail
ERASE %1
GOTO quit

:fail
ECHO.^G The move operation failed.
ECHO. Check your input names etc..

:quit
```

The file initially checks to ensure you have specified what to copy and where to copy it. If not, a help message is shown. The '^G' characters, **Alt+7**, cause the computer to beep when an error is encountered.

You can move file(s) from, and to, any drive or directory with **move.bat**, but you must spell out both the paths and filenames in both cases.

File Protection

It is very easy to accidentally delete files in a directory if you are in a hurry and not thinking of what you are doing. However, you can easily protect those files that will not need frequent updates, by making them READ ONLY with the ATTRIB command.

```
ATTRIB +R C:\config.sys
```

will make the file **config.sys** read only, in which case you will not be able to edit it without reversing the command, as follows:

```
ATTRIB -R C:\config.sys
```

The following batch file, **protect.bat**, gives you an easy way to implement and cancel protection of the two system files that you will need to edit fairly frequently, **config.sys** and **autoexec.bat**.

```
REM PROTECT.BAT
@ECHO OFF
IF "%1"=="1" GOTO protec
IF "%1"=="0" GOTO unprotec

:protec
ATTRIB +R C:\config.sys
ATTRIB +R C:\autoexec.bat
GOTO quit

:unprotec
ATTRIB -R C:\config.sys
ATTRIB -R C:\autoexec.bat

:quit
```

You could also add any other files that you want to protect to the lists in the above routine.

To make these files read only simply type **protect 1** at the DOS prompt. Test what has happened with the command:

```
ATTRIB C:\autoexec.bat
```

This should produce the following on the screen:

```
A    R    C:\AUTOEXEC.BAT
```

The 'R' indicates the read only attribute is set, as well as the archive. Whenever you need to edit one of the files, first type **protect 0** to cancel the protection. Don't forget to implement the protection again when you are finished.

Returning to the Current Directory

This routine is a little more involved than the previous ones. It solves the problem of making a batch file return control to the same drive and directory that was current when the batch file was called. Before using it you must create several files which will become 'permanent' to your system.

Place in your \BATCH directory the file **cdspace.bat** which will have only one line containing the text "CD " ("CD" followed by a space). An easy way to do this would be with the **addtext** utility covered at the end of Chapter 4, by typing at the prompt:

```
ADDTEXT C:\BATCH\cdspace.bat
CD
```

making sure that you follow the space with **F6** and <Enter>. Alternatively, **Edlin**, your text editor, or COPY CON could also be used to produce this file.

To enable the routine to keep track of the current drive you will need to add a file called **drive.tmp** to the root directory of all the drives on your system. Each of these files should hold the letter of the drive followed by a colon. For example, **drive.tmp** in C:\ would contain "C:" followed by <Enter> on the first line and "^Z" (**Ctrl+Z**, or **F6**) on the second.

To make sure these files do not get accidentally deleted you could set their attributes to read only, as described on the previous page. Once these files are installed enter **return.bat**:

```
REM RETURN.BAT
@ECHO OFF
REM Batch file to return you to the current
REM directory, on the current drive.
REM Can be used by placing:
REM      CALL return
REM at the beginning of another batch
REM file, and placing:
REM      CALL back
REM in that file when you want control
REM returned to the original location.
REM
REM
CD > C:\batch\return.tmp
COPY \drive.tmp + C:\batch\cdspace.bat
....+ C:\batch\return.tmp C:\batch\back.bat > nul
DEL C:\batch\return.tmp
```

The penultimate line of the file starts with **COPY \drive....** This has only been broken up to fit this book page. You should type it as one long line without the four dots.

The batch file works by opening the file **return.tmp** and placing the current path in it (without the drive letter in front). This is done by the command **CD > C:\batch\return.tmp**. The next long line builds the file **back.bat** in the C:\batch directory containing two lines; the current drive identifier (such as C:) on the first line and CD <current path> on the next.

To use this routine you should add the command **CALL return** to the beginning of any batch file that changes the current drive or directory. At the end of the file add the command **CALL back**, and control will be returned to the original directory when the batch file ends.

If your version of DOS is earlier than v3.3 the above two **CALL** commands will need to be changed to **COMMAND /C return.bat** and **COMMAND /C back.bat** respectively.

Extending the Current Path
Due to both the limited space in the DOS environment, and to aid system speed, it is not advisable to include too many directories on the permanent PATH statement in the **autoexec.bat** file. The following file cures this problem:

```
REM ADDPATH.BAT
@ECHO OFF
CLS
IF "%1"=="" GOTO message

:loop
SET PATH=%PATH%;%1
SHIFT
IF "%1"=="" GOTO quit
GOTO loop

:message
ECHO.This file adds more directories
ECHO.to the existing PATH when run.
ECHO.
ECHO.Example  %0 C:\lotus C:\WP51
ECHO.

:quit
ECHO.Path is now %PATH%
```

DOS does not include an easy way to extend the PATH without retyping the whole statement, but this file uses SET and the variable %PATH% to accomplish this. Any number of directories can be appended to the path (not exceeding 127 characters in all) by including them as parameters to the command **addpath**. Each one is appended in **:loop** - the SHIFT command makes the next parameter (%1) the first - and the looping process continues until all the parameters have been processed.

Increasing Environment Space

If you plan on using extensive additions to your PATH it may be wise to increase the default 256 bytes (in the case of DOS 5) of available space in your environment by including the following line in your **config.sys** file:

```
SHELL=C:\COMMAND.COM C:\ /P /E:512
```

This sets the environment to 512 bytes, which should be plenty, but you can increase it to a maximum of 32KB! The '/P' switch makes this copy of **command.com** permanent.

The above SHELL statement works with the command file in the root directory of the C: drive. If you wanted to keep your root directory clear, you could store **command.com** in the DOS directory and change the path in the SHELL command accordingly, say to C:\DOS\COMMAND.COM.

Simplifying the BACKUP Process

Everyone knows that you should backup the files on your hard disc at very regular intervals to avoid the horrors of lost data if the disc fails. Does everybody do it though? The DOS routines provided, BACKUP and RESTORE, can, to say the least, be very temperamental. Excellent commercial packages are available, but at a cost. You may find the following procedure both adequate and easy to carry out.

You should have original versions of your software programs on disc, so why spend a lot of time backing your programs up? If necessary, you can re-install them from the original discs. That probably takes care of most of your hard disc contents. The remaining data files obviously must be backed up. This will entail putting copies of every file onto floppy discs. The following batch file **bacup.bat** should make this a simple process. Once you are set up just run it once a day.

```
REM BACUP.BAT
@ECHO OFF
CLS
IF "%1"=="" GOTO message
ECHO.Backup of changed data files in %1
ECHO.and in all sub-directories of %1
ECHO.
ECHO.Place a FORMATTED disc in drive A:
ECHO.
PAUSE

:loop
XCOPY %1\*.* A: /s/e/v/m
IF ERRORLEVEL 5 GOTO error
IF ERRORLEVEL 4 GOTO full
IF ERRORLEVEL 1 GOTO nofiles
IF ERRORLEVEL 0 GOTO quit

:error
ECHO.^G There is a problem, check Drive A:
GOTO quit

:full
ECHO.^G Place another disc in Drive A:
PAUSE
GOTO loop

:nofiles
ECHO.No files found to backup
GOTO quit

:message
ECHO.^G No directory to backup specified
ECHO.
ECHO.Example  %0 C:\LOTUS123\DATA

:quit
```

This routine uses the external DOS command XCOPY which is a
very versatile command. Here, we force it to copy only files that
are new or have been updated since the last time it was run.
XCOPY reads as many files as will fit into RAM and then saves
them, one by one, to the destination disc. Hence, it operates
much faster than the COPY command.

In DOS v5.0, XCOPY does not copy hidden or system files,
whereas v3.3 version did. If your DOS is older than v3.3 you will

not have XCOPY at all, so maybe it is time to think about upgrading.

The **bacup** routine is simple to use. Let us assume your word processor files are stored in the C:\WP51\DOCS directory and maybe also in some subdirectories of this. Before using **bacup** for the first time, you will need to set the archive attribute of all the files in these directories. Make each directory in turn current and issue the command:

```
ATTRIB +A *.*
```

You will only need to do this once. Place a formatted disc in the A: drive and enter the command:

```
bacup C:\wp51\docs
```

After some initial messages the routine will copy all the files in the DOCS directory, as well as in all the subdirectories, to a series of discs in the A drive. The original subdirectory structure will be maintained on the floppy discs. As each file is copied XCOPY will cancel the archive attribute, so unless that file is modified, it will not be copied when next **bacup** is run. DOS itself sets the archive attribute, or flag, whenever a file is changed.

The operation of XCOPY is controlled by its switch parameters. In our routine the following switches are set:

/s   causes all subdirectories of the source path and their contents (except empty ones) to be copied

/e   copies empty subdirectories

/v   verifies the disc copy, by comparing the destination disc with the source

/m   copies only those files which have the archive flag set and then cancels the flag on all the files copied.

Other XCOPY switches which you could also use, are:

/a   does the same as /m but without altering the archive flag after copying

/d:*date*   copies only files that have been changed, or created, since the date specified

/p   prompts for confirmation before each file-copy

/w   makes XCOPY operation wait until any key is pressed - like a built-in pause command.

A Disc Cataloguing System

This file is for those people who have hundreds of files stored on an assortment of floppy discs and when they come to find a particular file have to search disc after disc. If this is a familiar scenario, read on. To get your discs organised you must first give each one a unique name. The simplest would be Disc 1, Disc 2 and so on, but with more ingenuity you could come up with a naming system to help indicate a disc's contents, or the time period during which it was used. If you keep each name less than 11 characters you can both write it on the outer label and use it with the LABEL command as below.

The batch file **diskcat.bat** shows a sorted directory listing of all the files on the disc in the A: drive on the screen, to remind you of its contents, and asks you for the disc label. Enter the disc name, or if the disc is already labelled press <Enter> followed by 'N' to the question "Delete current volume label (Y/N)" to keep the label. The disc name and a sorted list of all its contents is then appended to the file **diskcat.txt** in the C:\utils directory. The batch file will then loop through this routine for a series of discs in the A: drive, until the **F1** key is pressed to quit.

```
@ECHO OFF
REM DISKCAT.BAT
:loop
CLS
DIR A:\ /O /S
LABEL A:
DIR A:\ /O /S >> C:\UTILS\DISKLAB.TXT
CLS
ECHO.Disc catalogued. Press F1 to quit
ECHO.any other key to catalogue another
respond
IF ERRORLEVEL 59 IF NOT ERRORLEVEL 60 GOTO quit
GOTO loop


:quit
```

As it stands this routine will only work with DOS v5.0 and above. Previous versions of the DIR command have very limited switch options. For older DOS versions replace the DIR commands above with **DIR A: |SORT**. This will not list any subdirectories on the disc though.

When you have processed your discs simply load the text file **disklab.txt** into your word processor, format and print it, to give you a clear permanent record of the contents of all your discs. This stage you can make as detailed, or simple, as you want.

Turning Off the NUMLOCK Key

If, like us, you prefer to work with the NUMLOCK key switched off and your system leaves it on whenever it starts up, the following **Debug** routine may come in useful. As described previously, enter the following text into the file **nonumlok.scr** with your editor:

```
A
XOR AX,AX
MOV DS,AX
AND BYTE [417],DF
RET

R CX
A
N NONUMLOK.COM
W
Q
```

When you are happy your text is exactly the same as the above, save the file and from the C:\utils directory type the following:

```
DEBUG < nonumlok.scr
```

You should now have a small file **nonumlok.com**, which when run, turns off the NUMLOCK key. Simply place the command **nonumlok** in your autoexec.bat file and one of life's small irritations should be cured each time your system boots up.

APPENDIX A
THE DEBUG PROGRAM

In order to use the **Debug** program its command file **debug.com** must be in the currently logged directory or there must be a path to it, as the program is an external DOS file, in exactly the same way as **Edit** and **Edlin**. If you are using a floppy system, copy the **debug.com** file to your working floppy.

Debug can be used to look at memory locations, as well as change such memory locations. It provides a controlled test environment for binary and executable files (files with the .COM or .EXE extension). Here, we first start by looking at memory locations of loaded programs, before venturing further afield. In order to demonstrate how this can be done, we will use a four line **test.txt** file which you should create with the use of either the **Edit** screen editor or the **Edlin** line editor. The file should contain the following lines of text

```
first line of text
second line of text, edited
third line of text
fourth line of text
```

To start **Debug,** type its name followed by the name of the file you want to examine or change. In this case we type

```
C:\UTILS\>debug test.txt
-_
```

provided the file **test.txt** is to be found in the same directory as **Debug**. If it does, it causes **Debug** to respond with its own command prompt, in this case a hyphen (–).

The general form of starting **Debug** is:

debug *filespec arguments*

where *filespec* can be the full file specification, including drive, directory and filename. The *arguments* refer to parameters used by the program you want to examine.

When **Debug** loads a program into memory, it loads it starting at address 0100 hexadecimal (hex 0100, for short) in the lowest available segment. It also loads the number of bytes placed in memory into the CX register (more about this shortly).

If the filespec is not given when **Debug** is started, then it is assumed that you want to do one of the following:

(a) Examine current contents of memory,

(b) Load a program into memory using the **Debug Name** or **Load** commands

(c) Load absolute disc sectors into memory with the **Load** command.

The Dump Command

To examine the contents of memory while using **Debug**, type **d** (for dump), followed by 100 (the starting address on which to start the dump) and press <Enter>. This causes the first 128 bytes of memory starting from hex 100 to be displayed on the screen. In our case, the command

```
-d 0100
```

causes the following block to be displayed on the screen:

```
131B:0100  66 69 72 73 74 20 6C 69-6E 65 20 6F 66 20 74 65   first line of te
131B:0110  78 74 0D 0A 73 65 63 6F-6E 65 64 20 6C 69 6E 65 20   xt..second line
131B:0120  6F 66 20 74 65 78 74 2C-20 65 64 69 74 65 64 0D   of text, edited.
131B:0130  0A 74 68 69 72 64 20 6C-69 6E 65 20 6F 66 20 74   .third line of t
131B:0140  65 78 74 0D 0A 66 66 6F-75 72 74 68 20 6C 69 6E 65   ext..fourth line
131B:0150  20 6F 66 20 74 65 78 74-0D 0A 0D 0A 74 1C 33 C0    of text....t.3.
131B:0160  F6 06 C2 6F 20 74 09 FF-36 CA 6F 9A A3 76 E0 09   ...o t..6.o..v..
131B:0170  8B F0 E8 5D FD 75 03 96-EB C6 5E C3 8B C7 8B 1E   ...].u....^.....
```

Note that information is divided into three main areas:

Address	Byte value in Hex	ASCII characters
XXXX:0100	66 69 72 73 74 20 6C 69-6E 65 20 6F 66 20 74 65	first line of te

where 'address' refers to the address in memory, starting at hex 1DC8:0100 which is shown above as XXXX:0100 because the first part of the address (the XXXX portion of it) broadly defines the location of it in the computer's memory and is dependent on how much memory is installed and on how many resident programs happen to be loaded at the time. This part of the address will, more likely than not, be different on different computers, therefore it is shown above as XXXX.

Following the address, there is a block of 16 hexadecimal numbers representing the information held in memory so that location 0100, for example, holds the hex value of 66 (which is the ASCII value of the letter f), while location 0108 (just after the hyphen) holds the hex value of 6E (which is the ASCII value of the letter n). The hyphen here serves to divide the block of 16 bytes in half, for easy location - the first half contains bytes 0 to 7, while the second half contains bytes 8 to 15 inclusive.

The last area of the dump is the ASCII characters contained in the file we happen to be examining. Note that any bytes in that portion of memory having a hex value less than 32 are shown by **Debug** as periods within this last area. Thus, 0D (carriage return - decimal 13) and 0A (line feed - decimal 10) which occur in memory locations 0112 and 0113, respectively, are shown as .. in the second line of the ASCII character portion of the dump. It is worth your while spending some time examining this dump. For example, try to locate the positions of the 'spaces' in the text which have the hex value of 20.

The dump command can also be used without any parameters (i.e. the starting memory location taken as hex 0100 in our previous example). If this had been done the first time we issued the dump command, after starting **Debug**, then dumping would have started at memory location 0100 anyway, as this is the default starting value for a dump of memory. The next time **d** is typed, then the contents of the next 128 bytes of memory are dumped, from hex 0180 to 01FF.

The dump command can also be used to display a specific number of bytes. If this is required, then the command must be followed by the starting and ending address of memory. That is,

d *start stop*

Thus, to display the first line of our example, you must type

-d 0100 010F

and press <Enter>.

Another form of the command, in controlling the number of bytes to be displayed, is by specifying the starting location and the length (L) of the required bytes. For example, the first line of our example can be displayed by typing

-d 0100 L 10

In the above command, we used uppercase L to specify length, as the lower-case letter could easily by mistaken as the numeral 1. The number of bytes to be displayed above follows L and is hex 10 which is decimal 16.

The Fill Command
In the dump of the file **test.txt**, we showed the display with certain values after location hex 015A. These values might be different with your computer, because it depends on what happened to be loaded in these locations at the time. We can achieve a more aesthetic result with the use of the **f** (for fill) command. The command takes the following form:

```
-f 0100 0180 0
```

which means 'fill memory locations hex 0100 to 0180 with 0'. Do this and verify it by following it with

```
-d 0100
```

Now all the displayed locations hold the hex value 0 and the ASCII character part of the dump contains only periods.
  The general form of the fill command is as follows:

```
f range list
```

If a *range* is specified that contains more bytes than the number of values in the *list*, **Debug** uses the *list* repeatedly until it fills all bytes in the *range*. If the *list* contains more values than the number of bytes in the *range*, **Debug** ignores the extra values in the *list*.

The Load Command
We can now 'load' our **test.txt** file from the buffer into these zeroed locations with the L (for Load) command. Again we use an uppercase letter to avoid confusion by mistaking it for the numeral 1. Thus, typing

```
-L 0100
```

and pressing <Enter>, loads our file from the buffer. To display the result, simply type

```
-d 0100
```

and press <Enter>.

Now you will get a 'cleaner' display of the dump, as the empty memory locations are now filled with 0s.

Note the very last byte of the file in location hex 15A; it contains the value 1A which is what you get when you type **Ctrl+Z**, and represents the end-of-file marker.

The Name Command
The **n** (for name) command is used to assign a filename to **Debug** to use later with the load and write commands. When **Debug** is started without specifying a file, the name command must be used in order to set a file. For example,

```
-n file
-L
```

The name command can also be used to supply a program that is to be used by **Debug** with information essential to its proper execution. For example, we can use the name command to name a file that requires some data by

```
-n file1.com datafile
-L
```

To take up the earlier example of our file **test.txt** and the requirement of an uncluttered display, we can achieve the same thing by simply typing

```
-f 0100 0180 0
-n test.txt
-L 0100
-d 0100
```

causes the following display to appear on your screen:

```
131B:0100  66 69 72 73 74 20 6C 69-6E 65 20 6F 66 20 74 65   first line of te
131B:0110  78 74 0D 0A 73 65 63 6F-6E 65 20 6C 69 6E 65 20   xt..second line
131B:0120  6F 66 20 74 65 78 74 2C-20 65 64 69 74 65 64 0D   of text, edited.
131B:0130  0A 74 68 69 72 64 20 6C-69 6E 65 20 6F 66 20 74   .third line of t
131B:0140  65 78 74 0D 0A 66 6F 75-72 74 68 20 6C 69 6E 65   ext..fourth line
131B:0150  20 6F 66 20 74 65 78 74-0D 0A 0D 0A 00 00 00 00    of text........
131B:0160  00 00 00 00 00 00 00 00-00 00 00 00 00 00 00 00   ................
131B:0170  00 00 00 00 00 00 00 00-00 00 00 00 00 00 00 00   ................
-
```

The Enter Command

The **e** (for name) command allows us to enter data directly into memory as byte values or as a string of characters. The general form of the command is

   e *address list*

where the values in *list* replace the contents of one or more bytes starting at *address*.

   Again, assuming that the **test.txt** file has been loaded by **Debug**, we can substitute the existing values in memory starting at address hex 0120 with the string "edited by debug", and display the result, with the following commands:

```
-e 0120 "edited by debug"
-d 0100
```

What is now displayed on your screen is as follows:

```
131B:0100  66 69 72 73 74 20 6C 69-6E 65 20 6F 66 20 74 65   first line of te
131B:0110  78 74 0D 0A 73 65 63 6F-6E 64 20 6C 69 6E 65 20   xt..second line
131B:0120  65 64 69 74 65 64 20 62-79 20 64 65 62 75 67 0D   edited by debug.
131B:0130  0A 74 68 69 72 64 20 6C-69 6E 65 20 6F 66 20 74   .third line of t
131B:0140  65 78 74 0D 0A 66 6F 75-72 74 68 20 6C 69 6E 65   ext..fourth line
131B:0150  20 6F 66 20 74 65 78 74-0D 0A 0D 0A 00 00 00 00    of text........
131B:0160  00 00 00 00 00 00 00 00-00 00 00 00 00 00 00 00   ................
131B:0170  00 00 00 00 00 00 00 00-00 00 00 00 00 00 00 00   ................
-
```

The same changes could be achieved by typing the actual values we want to change in hex. For example, typing

```
-e 0120 65 64 69 74 65 64 20 62 79 20 64 65 62 75 67
```

produces the same change as "edited by debug"!

   If the *list* parameter is omitted, then **Debug** displays the address, its contents, and a period, and waits for input.

The Write Command

The **w** (for write) command writes an area of memory to the file was either last loaded by **Debug** or most recently named with the name command. Thus, we can save the changed file of our example above by first naming a file we would like to save the results of the changes in and then writing to that file.

   For example, assuming that the **test.txt** file has been changed with the edit command, we could type

```
-n test1.txt
-w
```

which will save the changes in the **test1.txt** file, leaving the old **test.txt** file unaltered.

The general form of the write command is:

   w *start*

where *start* is the starting address in memory from which a number of bytes are written to the file. If 'start' is omitted, **Debug** starts at address 0100.

When the write command is executed, **Debug** informs you of the total number of bytes (in hexadecimal) it wrote to the file.

In this case, the message

```
Writing 0005B bytes
```

appears on the screen.

This number is the same as that placed in the CX register when the original file was loaded into memory. In this case, the operation will be correct since we have not changed the actual length of the file. However, had we changed the overall length of the file by, say, appending information to it, then before writing the changes to file, we must change the value held in the CX register to the new length.

Registers

The Intel Central Processing Unit (CPU) family that includes the 8086, 8088, 80x86, are similar in many respects. All these processors can handle 16-bit data internally and can, therefore, accept a common set of instructions. In addition, all these processors communicate with the outside world with a 16-bit data bus, with the exception of the 8088 which operates with an 8-bit data bus, thus making it slower.

The CPUs provide special internal 'memory locations', called registers. For the 8088-80286 CPUs there are 14 such registers each being 16-bits wide, and for the 80386 (or higher) CPUs there are 16, 32-bit registers. Since these registers are integrated within the processor chip, they can manipulate information very quickly. These registers are subdivided into groups according to the tasks they normally perform. The following two tables list the names, length and normal tasks associated with the registers.

TABLE A-1 Names and Tasks of 16-bit Registers

15	7	0	
AH	AL		AX, Accumulator
DH	DL		DX, Data
CH	CL		CX, Count
BH	BL		BX, Base
BP			Base Pointer
SI			Source Index
DI			Destination Index
SP			Stack Pointer
CS			Code Segment
DS			Data Segment
SS			Stack Segment
ES			Extra Segment
IP			Instruction Pointer
Flags			Status flags: NV UP EI PL NZ NA PO NC

The first four of the CPU registers are referred to as the general purpose registers AX, BX, CX, and DX. These can be used as either 16-bit or 8-bit registers, which is why they are shown in two halves; the high half (H) and the low half (L). Each half can be addressed separately.

Following the general purpose registers are two pointer and two index registers, which serve as pointers to locate data in main memory. These are referred to as SP (stack pointer), BP (Base pointer), SI (source index), and DI (destination index).

Since all the CPU registers are 16-bits long, this means that any such register can only access 2^{16} = 65,536 (or 64K) bytes of memory. To overcome this limitation, any of these registers can be combined with an appropriate segment register to address much larger chunks of memory, the actual size being dependent on the total number of combined bits.

For example, SS and SP are combined for stack operations, while CS and IP are combined to locate the next instruction. Mostly, these combinations are arranged within the CPU by default. The maximum addressable memory, when two 16-bit registers are combined end-to-end, corresponds to 2^{20} bytes which is one megabyte. Such memory addressing is called the 'effective address'. The segment register is combined with the offset register in the following way.

Suppose that the CS register contains 53C2h and the IP register contains 107Ah, then the physical address will be

```
     53C20h        Segment times 10h (16 decimal)
  +   107Ah        Offset
     ----------------
     54C9Ah
```

Therefore, if the contents of CS and IP were set to address the highest accessible address (0FFFFFh) then CS would contain F000h and IP would contain FFFFh (CS could contain FFFFh and IP contain 000Fh). In other words, there is more than one way of defining a physical memory address.

In the case of the 80386 (or higher) processor, the CPU registers are 32-bits long and addresses may be formed using a 16-bit segment and a 32-bit offset. This gives a maximum possible address space of 2^{48} or a massive 4 gigabytes of memory (this addressing is only permitted when the CPU is operating in 'protected' mode, such as under Microsoft Windows 3.0 or higher and other multitasking environments. A description of this mode of operation is beyond the scope of this book.)

The table on the next page shows the size and general usage of each register in the 80386 (or higher) CPUs.

TABLE A-2 Names and Tasks of 32-bit Registers

31	23	15	7	0	
			AH	AL	EAX, Accumulator
			DH	DL	EDX, Data
			CH	CL	ECX, Count
			BH	BL	EBX, Base
			BP		Base Pointer
			SI		Source Index
			DI		Destination Index
			SP		Stack Pointer
			CS		Code Segment
			DS		Data Segment
			SS		Stack Segment
			ES		Extra Segment
			FS		Extra Segment
			GS		Extra Segment
			I P		Instruction Pointer
			Flags		Flags

The Register Command:
The register command allows us to display the names and contents of the registers. To display all the registers, type

   -r

which will cause **Debug** to respond with

```
AX=0000  BX=0000  CX=005B  DX=0000  SP=FFEE  BP=0000  SI=0000  DI=0000
DS=131B  ES=131B  SS=131B  CS=131B  IP=0100  NU UP EI PL NZ NA PO NC
131B:0100 66            DB     66
-
```

assuming that file **test1.txt** was in memory at the time. Note the contents of the CX register which is 005B, the length of our file.

To change the contents of a register, type the register command, followed by the name of the register. Thus, in the case of the CX register, type

```
-r cx
```

which causes **Debug** to repeat the name of the register and the current value held in it (in hex), and then prompt you for a new value by displaying a colon. For example,

```
CX 005B
:_
```

At that point we can type the new length of the file in hex, or press <Enter> to abort.

Appending to a File

As an example, let us add the string "Last line addition" to the end of the previous file. We start with address 15A which contains the value 1A representing the Ctrl-Z at the end of the file. This is not needed and can be overwritten. Thus, typing

```
-e 15A "Last line addition"
```

adds 18 (decimal) bytes to the length of the file which was hex 005B (decimal 91) - look up Table 1 in Chapter 1 for conversion of decimal to hex, and vice versa.

Since we have already overwritten the contents of location 15A, the new length is 91-1+18 = 108 bytes, occupying locations 0100 through to 016B. Now add a carriage return (0D) and a line feed (0A) to the end of the additional line by typing

```
-e 016C 0D 0A
```

which now makes the length to 110 (decimal) bytes or hex 6E.

We now need to change the contents of the CX register, and to this end we type

```
-r cx
```

which causes **Debug** to display the present contents of the register and prompt for the change, which we type in as 6E, as follows:

```
CX 005B
:6E
```

Before we write the present contents of memory to file, we can name a new file with the **n** command, say **test2.txt**, by typing

```
-n test2.txt
-w
```

which causes **Debug** to respond with

```
Writing 0006E bytes
```

A screen dump of the reloaded file is shown below, which verifies what we have been discussing above.

```
131B:0100  66 69 72 73 74 20 6C 69-6E 65 20 6F 66 20 74 65   first line of te
131B:0110  78 74 0D 0A 73 65 63 6F-6E 64 20 6C 69 6E 65 20   xt..second line
131B:0120  65 64 69 74 65 64 20 62-79 20 64 65 62 75 67 0D   edited by debug.
131B:0130  0A 74 68 69 72 64 20 6C-69 6E 65 20 6F 66 20 74   .third line of t
131B:0140  65 78 74 0D 0A 66 6F 75-72 74 68 20 6C 69 6E 65   ext..fourth line
131B:0150  20 6F 66 20 74 65 78 74-0D 0A 4C 61 73 74 20 6C    of text..Last l
131B:0160  69 6E 65 20 61 64 64 69-74 69 6F 6E 0D 0A 00 00   ine addition....
131B:0170  00 00 00 00 00 00 00 00-00 00 00 00 00 00 00 00   ................
-
```

The Assemble Command
The general form of the **a** (for assemble) command is

   a *address*

where *address* is the memory location we want to start **Debug** assembling the statement we enter. If the address parameter is omitted, then **Debug** starts assembling with the location following the last location assembled. If the assemble command had not been used since starting **Debug**, the assembling starts with the location pointed to by CS:IP which is CS:0100 if no file is loaded or if the file loaded is a .COM file.

When all statements have been entered, the <Enter> (or <Return>) key must be pressed to provide an empty line which signifies the end location for the assembly.

All numeric values must be entered as 1 to 4 hex digits. Prefix assembler mnemonics must be entered in front of the operation codes (called opcodes) to which they refer, but can also be entered on a separate line. In general, a line of source code is divided into the following four sections:

Label   Mnemonic   Operand   Comment

The 'label' is a symbolic reference to the memory location where the next instruction is located, normally used as the target of a jump or subroutine call. A label can contain alphanumeric characters and the underscore character, but the first character must be a letter. A colon is typed at the end of a label to indicate that this label will be referenced only within the current segment of code.

The 'mnemonic' symbolises a CPU instruction, such as MOV (for move), while the 'operand' refers to the operation to be executed, such as AH,02 (AH referring to the destination, with hex 02 referring to the source).

The 'comment' symbolises an explanation of the instruction and must be preceded by a semi-colon.

Thus, the line

```
begin: MOV AH,02 ; move hex 02 into register AH
```

represents one possible line of assembler instruction.

Below is a list of the mnemonics, together with their meaning, which we will be using later in this book.

TABLE A-3 List of Common Assembler Mnemonics

ADD	Add destination to source
CMP	Compare destination to source
INT	Call interrupt type
IRET	Interrupt return
JMP	Jump to target
JNZ	Jump if not zero
JZ	Jump if zero
MOV	Move into destination the source

The GO Command

The **g** (for go) command executes the program in memory. Its general form is:

g =*address1 address2*

where *address1* is the address where **Debug** begins execution and changes both the CS and IP registers, while *address2* sets break-points which stop program execution. If both addresses are omitted, then **Debug** executes the program normally. If the segment is not specified, then **Debug** replaces the value in the IP register with *address1*. The equal sign must be included with *address1*. When program execution reaches a break-point, the **Debug** displays the registers, flags, and decoded instructions of the next instruction ready for execution.

The **go** command uses the IRET instruction to cause a jump to the program under test. When a program is completed, then you must reload the program before you can execute it or debug it again.

The Unassemble Command

The **u** (for unassemble) command, converts memory back to assembly language mnemonics (disassembles bytes) along with address and byte values. The display of a disassembled code looks just like a file ready for assembly. The format is:

u *address*
or
u *range*

where *address* is the address at which disassembly starts with the location pointed to by CS:IP. If *address* is omitted, then **Debug** starts converting code after the last location disassembled. If *range* is omitted, **Debug** disassembles 20 hex bytes.

The Quit Command

The **q** (for quit) command can be used to leave **Debug** and return to DOS without saving any changes made. To save the contents of memory to file, the write command must be issued before the quit command.

There are a lot more commands in **Debug**, but what has been presented here is more than enough for what we need.

APPENDIX B
SYSTEM CONFIGURATION

If you are using a computer with a hard disc, then it is assumed that you have structured it in such a way as to hold all the DOS external command files in the subdirectory \DOS, all the batch files in the subdirectory \BATCH, and that you hold the other utility programs we develop in this book, in a subdirectory called \UTILS.

The Config.sys File

This file (located on the root directory of the boot-up drive) allows you to configure your computer to your needs, as commands held in it are executed during booting up the system. The easiest way to amend this system file is with the use of either the **Edit** screen editor (available only to users of DOS 5), or the **Edlin** line editor (available to users of all other versions of DOS), as discussed in the preceding chapters.

If you are setting up your system for the first time, you will need to change the **config.sys** file that is created for you by the SETUP program, because it might not include all the commands you will require to run your system efficiently. To view the contents of the file, use the **type** command followed by the filename, at the system prompt.

The commands included in the **config.sys** file below, could be quite adequate for versions of DOS prior to MS-DOS 5.0.

```
SHELL=C:\DOS\COMMAND.COM C:\DOS\ /E:256 /P
DEVICE=C:\DOS\ANSI.SYS
COUNTRY=044,,C:\DOS\COUNTRY.SYS
BREAK=ON
FILES=30
BUFFERS=30
LASTDRIVE=E
```

Commands in **config.sys** file for DOS versions prior to DOS 5.0.

Do remember that any changes made to this file only take effect after re-booting which can be achieved by pressing either the reset button on the system unit of your computer, or the 3 keys **Ctrl+Alt+Del** simultaneously.

If, on the other hand, you are running DOS 5, then the above commands will not be adequate enough. Exactly what command you include in your **config.sys** file will depend on the type of processor in your machine and the available size of extended memory in your system.

The list below, contains commands that you can include within your **config.sys** file when running DOS 5 on a 386 processor machine with at least 3 Mbytes of RAM.

```
SHELL=C:\DOS\COMMAND.COM C:\DOS\ /E:256 /P
DEVICE=C:\DOS\HIMEM.SYS
DOS=HIGH,UMB
DEVICE=C:\DOS\EMM386.EXE RAM I=B000-B7FF,I=E000-EFFF
DEVICE=C:\DOS\ANSI.SYS
DEVICEHIGH=C:\DOS\SMARTDRV.SYS 1024 128
DEVICEHIGH=C:\DOS\RAMDRIVE.SYS 512 /E
DEVICEHIGH=C:\DOS\SETVER.EXE
COUNTRY=044,,C:\DOS\COUNTRY.SYS
BREAK=ON
FILES=30
BUFFERS=30
LASTDRIVE=E
```

Commands in **config.sys** file for DOS 5 version on a 386 machine.

Again, do remember that any changes made to this file only take effect after re-booting which can be achieved by pressing the reset button, or the 3 keys **Ctrl+Alt+Del** simultaneously.

Configuration Commands:
A brief explanation of the configuration commands, which can be included within the **config.sys** file, is given below:

BREAK   By including the command BREAK=ON in the **config.sys** file, you can use the key combination **Ctrl+C** (hold the key marked Ctrl down and press C) or **Ctrl+Break**, to interrupt MS-DOS I/O functions.

BUFFERS   MS-DOS allocates memory space in RAM, called buffers, to store whole sectors of data being read from disc, each of 512 bytes in size. If more data are required, MS-DOS first searches the buffers before searching the disc, which speeds up operations.

90

The number of buffers can be changed by using:

BUFFERS=n

where n can be a number from 1 to 99. However, as each buffer requires an additional 0.5 Kbyte of RAM, the number you should use is dependent on the relative size between the package you are using and your computer's RAM. Best results are obtained by choosing between 10-30 buffers.

COUNTRY   MS-DOS displays dates according to the US format which is month/day/year. To change this to day/month/year, use the command

COUNTRY=044

where 044 is for U.K. users.

Non U.K. users can substitute their international telephone country code for the 044. The default value is 001, for the USA.

DEVICE   MS-DOS includes its own standard device drivers which allow communication with your keyboard, screen and discs. However, these drivers can be extended to allow other devices to be connected by specifying them in the **config.sys** file. Example of these are:

DEVICE=ANSI.SYS

which loads alternative screen and keyboard drivers for ANSI support - features of which are required by some commercial software.

DEVICE=SETVER.EXE

which sets the version number that MS-DOS v5 reports to a program. You can use this command at the system prompt to display the version table, which lists names of programs and the number of the MS-DOS version with which they are designed to run, or add a program that has not been updated to MS-DOS 5.

DEVICE=MOUSEAnn.SYS

allows the use of specific mouse devices.

DEVICE=VDISK.SYS n

allows you to specify the size n in Kbytes (default 64) of RAM to be used as an extra very fast virtual disc. With computers which have more than 640 Kbytes of RAM, the option /E can be used after n in the command to allocate the specified memory size from the extra area of RAM.

DEVICE=DRIVER.SYS

allows you to connect an external disc drive.

DEVICE=EGA.SYS

provides mouse support for EGA modes.

DEVICE=COMn.SYS

specifies asynchronous drivers for the serial ports, where for n=01 specifies an IBM PC AT COM device, and n=02 specifies an IBM PS/2 COM device.

DEVICEHIGH Loads device drivers into the upper memory area.

DOS Sets the area of RAM where MS-DOS will be located, and specifies whether to use the upper memory area. The command takes the form:

DOS=HIGH

DRIVPARM Sets characteristics of a disc drive.

FCBS Specifies the number of FCBs that can be opened concurrently. The command takes the following form:

FCBS=x,y

where x specifies the total number of files by
FCBs, from 1 to 255, that can be opened at
any one time (the default value being 4), and y
specifies the number of opened files (from
1-255) that cannot be closed automatically by
MS-DOS if an application tries to open more
than x files.

FILES   MS-DOS normally allows 8 files to be opened
at a time. However, some software such as
relational databases, might require to refer to
more files at any given time. To accommodate
this, MS-DOS allows you to change this
default value by using:

FILES=n

where n can be a number from 8 to the
maximum required by your application which
usually is 20, although the maximum allowable
is 99.

INSTALL   This command runs a terminate-and-stay-
resident (TSR) program, such as FASTOPEN,
KEYB, NLSFUNC, or SHARE while MS-DOS
reads the **config.sys** file. The command takes
the following form:

INSTALL=filespec[params]

where *params* specifies the optional line to
pass to the *filespec* which must be
FASTOPEN.EXE, KEYB.EXE, NLSFUNC.EXE
or SHARE.EXE.

LASTDRIVE   This command is used if additional drives are
to be connected to your system, or you are
sharing a hard disc on a network. The
command takes the form:

LASTDRIVE=x

where x is a letter from A to Z (default E).

REM   REM followed by any string, allows remarks to
            be entered in the **config.sys**.

SHELL   Manufacturers of some micros provide a 'front
            end' or an alternative Command Processor to
            COMMAND.COM as real-mode command-line
            processor. To invoke this, the command
            SHELL must be included within the **config.sys**
            file. The command takes the form:

            SHELL=FRONTEND.COM

            where FRONTEND is the name of the
            alternative Command Processor. The default
            value of SHELL is COMMAND.COM.

STACKS   Sets the amount of RAM that MS-DOS
            reserves for processing hardware interrupts.

SWITCHES   Specifies the use of conventional keyboard
            functions even though an enhanced keyboard
            is installed.

The Autoexec.bat File

This is a special batch file (located on the root directory of the
boot-up drive) that MS-DOS looks for during the last stages of
booting up and if it exists, the commands held in it will be
executed. One such command is the KEYB xx which configures
keyboards for the appropriate national standard, with xx
indicating the country. For the U.K., the command becomes
KEYB UK, and you will need to execute it if your keyboard is
marked with the double quotes sign on the 2 key and/or the @
sign over the single quotes key and/or the £ sign over the 3 key.

The easiest way to amend this system file is with the use of
either **Edit** or **Edlin**, as discussed earlier. If you are setting up
your system for the first time, you will need to change the
autoexec.bat file that is created for you by the SETUP
program, because it might not include all the commands you
will require to run your system efficiently. If your system has
been implemented by, say, your computer staff, do not edit this
file or use **Edit** or **Edlin** to look at its contents, unless you have
to and you know precisely what you are doing, as the file

contains entries that MS-DOS uses to define specific operating attributes. To view the contents of the file, use the **type** command followed by the filename, at the system prompt.

The commands included in the **autoexec.bat** file below, could be quite adequate for versions of DOS prior to DOS 5.0.

```
@ECHO OFF
SET COMSPEC=C:\DOS\COMMAND.COM
VERIFY OFF
PATH C:\DOS;C:\WINDOWS;C:\BATCH;C:\UTILS
C:\WINDOWS\mouse.COM
C:\DOS\APPEND \Batch
C:\DOS\KEYB UK,,C:\DOS\KEYBOARD.SYS /ID:166
C:\DOS\GRAPHICS GRAPHICS
PROMPT $P$G
SET TEMP=D:\
ECHO H E L L O ... This is your PC using
VER
```

Commands in **autoexec.bat** file for DOS versions prior to DOS 5.0.

Exactly what command you include in your **autoexec.bat** file when running DOS 5 will depend on the type of processor in your machine and the available size of extended memory in your system. The list below is suitable for a 386 processor machine with at least 3 Mbytes of RAM.

```
@ECHO OFF
SET COMSPEC=C:\DOS\COMMAND.COM
C:\WINDOWS\SMARTDRV.EXE
VERIFY OFF
PATH C:\DOS;C:\WINDOWS;C:\BATCH;C:\UTILS
LOADHIGH C:\WINDOWS\mouse.COM
LH C:\DOS\APPEND \Batch
LH C:\DOS\KEYB UK,,C:\DOS\KEYBOARD.SYS /ID:166
LH C:\DOS\GRAPHICS GRAPHICS
LH C:\DOS\DOSKEY
PROMPT $P$G
SET TEMP=D:\
ECHO H E L L O ... This is your PC using
VER
```

Commands in **autoexec.bat** file for DOS 5 version on a 386 machine.

Do remember, that any changes made to the **autoexec.bat** file only take effect after typing

```
autoexec
```

at the system prompt, or when re-booting the system by either pressing the reset button on your computer's system unit, or the three keys **Ctrl+Alt+Del** simultaneously.

Other commands within the **autoexec.bat** file carry out the following functions:

Command	*Function*
APPEND	Enables programs to open data files in specified directories from the current directory.
ECHO	Displays messages on screen, or turns the echo feature on or off.
GRAPHICS	Allows MS-DOS to print on a graphics printer the information appearing on the screen. The parameter GRAPHICS indicates that printer is an IBM printer.
KEYB	Identifies the type of keyboard connected to your system.
MOUSE	Loads the mouse driver that comes with the mouse device.
PATH	Sets a search path for executable files.
PROMPT	Changes the appearance of the MS-DOS command prompt. The parameter $P forces the display of the current drive and path, while the parameter &G displays the greater-than sign (>).
SET	Allows an environment variable named TEMP to be associated with the string C:\WINDOWS\TEMP. This is the subdirectory where Microsoft Windows creates and later deletes temporary files.
VER	Displays the version of MS-DOS running on your system.
VERIFY	Turns on/off verification that files are written correctly to disc.

APPENDIX C
PRINTER COMMANDS

This Appendix lists some of the more useful printer commands of the Epson EX800 compatible and the HP LaserJet III compatible printers. The commands are categorised under three printer functions; 'printer control', 'typeface', and 'format'.

The commands use the following conventions:

^G   as in Table C-1, is obtained by holding down the **Ctrl** key and pressing the upper case letter G.

{ESC}   represents the ASCII character 27 (called 'Escape') and if you are using the screen editor **Edit** you should enter it by first typing **Ctrl+P**, then pressing the <Esc> key which causes the left arrow (←) to appear on the screen. If, on the other hand, you are using the line editor **Edlin**, then enter it by first typing **Ctrl+V** (which displays as ^V) followed by [.

O   as in ^O in Table C-2, represents uppercase letter o.

l   as in {ESC}ln in Table C-3, is the lower case letter L (not 1).

n   represents a number (e.g. number of columns in above example).

0   as in {ESC}0 in Table C-3, represents character zero.

TABLE C-1 List of Common Printer Control Commands
==

Function	Epson	HP III
Bell - Sounds the printer beep	^G	^G
Cariage Return	^M	^M
Form feed - advances paper to top of next page (with the HP, it also ejects page)	^L	^L
Horizontal TAB	^I	{ESC}&anR
Line feed	^J	^J
Reset - resets printer to standard settings (with HP it also ejects a page)	{ESC}@	{ESC}E

TABLE C-2 List of Common Printer Typeface Commands
===

Function	Epson	HP III
Character height - Points		{ESC}(nV
Condensed start	^O	
Condensed stop	^R	
Double-strike start	{ESC}G	
Double-strike stop	{ESC}H	
Expanded start - one line only	^N	
Expanded start - until stopped	{ESC}W1	
Expanded stop - stops ^N only	^T	
Expanded stop - stops {ESC}W1 only	{ESC}W0	
Italic start	{ESC}4	
Pitch (characters per inch)		{ESC}(snH
Spacing - Proportional	{ESC}p2	{ESC}(s1P
Spacing - Fixed	{ESC}p1	{ESC}(s0P
Style Italic	{ESC}4	{ESC}(s1S
Style Upright - normal	{ESC}5	{ESC}(s0S
Style Subscript start	{ESC}S1	
Style Superscript start	{ESC}S0	
Style Subscript/superscript stop	{ESC}T	
Stroke weight Light		{ESC}(s-3B
Stroke weight Medium		{ESC}(0B
Stroke weight Bold		{ESC}(s3B
Symbol set to PC-8		{ESC}(10U)
Symbol set to Roman-8		{ESC}(8U
Typeface Line Printer		{ESC}(s0T
Typeface Boldface start	{ESC}E	
Typeface Boldface stop	{ESC}F	
Typeface Pica	{ESC}P	{ESC}(s1T
Typeface Elite	{ESC}M	{ESC}(s2T
Typeface Courier		{ESC}(s3T
Typeface Helvetica		{ESC}(s4T
Typeface Times Roman		{ESC}(s5T
Underline start	{ESC}-1	{ESC}&d0D
Underline stop	{ESC}-0	{ESC}&d@

TABLE C-3 List of Common Printer Format Commands
===

Function	Epson	HP III
Line spacing to $1/_8$ inch	{ESC}2	
Line spacing to $1/_6$ inch	{ESC}0	
Line spacing in n multiples of $1/_{72}$"	{ESC}An	
Line spacing in n multiples of $1/_{216}$"	{ESC}3n	
Line spacing to specified lines per inch		{ESC}&lnD
Margin Left - sets margin to specified nth column	{ESC}ln	{ESC}&anL
Margin Right - sets margin to specified nth column	{ESC}Qn	{ESC}&anM
Margins Clear - both Left and Right		{ESC}9
Motion index Horizontal		{ESC}&knH
Motion index Vertical - sets space between rows to specified multiple of $1/_{48}$"		{ESC}&lnC
Page length to specified number of inches	{ESC}C0n	
Page length to specified number of lines	{ESC}Cn	{ESC}&lnP
Page orientation Portrait n=0, Landscape n=1		{ESC}&lnO

INDEX

NOTES

NOTES

NOTES

NOTES

MAKING MS-DOS WORK FOR YOU

COMPANION DISC

This book contains many pages of batch file listings. There is no reason why you should spend many hours typing them in, unless you are learning to type and need the practice.

The COMPANION DISC for this book comes with all the listings, organised into a separate subdirectory for each chapter. It is available in both 3.5-inch and 5.25-inch formats.

COMPANION DISCS for all books produced by either, or both, authors, with the same publisher, are also available and are listed at the front of this book. Make sure you specify the book number with your order (eg BP 319)

ORDERING INSTRUCTIONS

To obtain your copy use the order blank below and enclose a cheque, payable to **P.R.M.Oliver**, or a postal order.

Book No.	Book Name	Unit Price	Total Price
BP 319	Making MS-DOS Work for You	£2.50	
		£2.50	
		£2.50	
Name .... Address		Sub-total	£.............
		P & P	£.... 0.45
		Total Due	£.............
Disc Format 3.5-inch....... 5.25-inch.......			
Send to: P.R.M.Oliver, CSM, Pool, Redruth, Cornwall, TR15 3SE			